The Englishman's Italian Books
1550-1700

Publications of the A. S. W. Rosenbach Fellowship in Bibliography

William Charvat, *Literary Publishing in America: 1790-1850*

Curt F. Bühler, *The Fifteenth-Century Book: The Scribes, the Printers, the Decorators*

Archer Taylor, *General Subject-Indexes since 1548*

Cass Canfield, *The Publishing Experience*

John L. Lievsay, *The Englishman's Italian Books, 1550-1700*

En virtute suâ contentus, nobilis arte ,
Italus ore, Anglus pectore, vterq̃ opere
Floret adhuc, et adhuc florebit; floreat vltra
FLORIVS, hâc specie floridus, optat amans.

Gul: Hole sculp: Tam fælix vtinam.

Portrait of Giovanni Florio from Michel de Montaigne's *Essayes*
(second edition, 1613). Reproduced by permission from a copy in The
Folger Shakespeare Library.

The Englishman's Italian Books
1550-1700

by

JOHN L. LIEVSAY

A. S. W. Rosenbach Fellow in Bibliography

UNIVERSITY OF PENNSYLVANIA PRESS
PHILADELPHIA

PREFACE

The three lectures here printed were delivered at the Library of the University of Pennsylvania on March 18, March 25, and April 1, 1969, for the A.S.W. Rosenbach Lectures in Bibliography. Except for minor changes in phrasing, they are presented now in substantially their original form. I have, however, taken the opportunity provided by the printed volume to add to the second lecture several further remarks omitted in the first instance under restrictions of time. Here and there, also, I have transferred from the notes to the text statistical matter more acceptable to the eye than to the ear.

To the Selection Committee of the Rosenbach Lectures series I express my appreciation of the signal honor conferred by their invitation; and to Dr. Neda Westlake and her staff my sincere thanks for arranging a most judiciously chosen exhibit of books pertinent to the theme of the lectures.

J. L. L.

Washington, D.C.
July 12, 1969

CONTENTS

ILLUSTRATIONS

The Englishman's Italian Books
1550-1700

I

English Printers, Italian Texts

A sixteenth-century Italian writer who knew a great deal about practically everything and made no bones about displaying his knowledge has, in one of his encyclopedic publications, a discourse concerning printers. He sees the invention of printing as a sort of Angelica's ring which has broken the spell of ancient ignorance and ushered his times into the realms of light, opening the eyes of the blind and giving new vision to the ignorant, enabling all to distinguish gold from lead, roses from thorns, grain from chaff, good from evil. An art, he says—and we can only agree—truly rare, stupendous, and miraculous. He has other words of praise for the art and mystery of printing, seasoned with a sprinkling of facts about its history and practice, all pointing toward his conclusion that Printers are Pretty Admirable Fellows. Then he ends, characteristically, with the satiric observation that they have in them no faults except that they are occasionally sleepyheaded over corrections, they are high handed in dealing with other people's texts, they often bestow great pains on useless topics, and are unconcerned and negligent with more profitable matters.[1]

He was thinking, of course, about printers in his own Italy, some of whom—the Aldi, the Gioliti, the Giunti, among others—he names and praises. If he was aware that printing was practiced in England, he does not mention the fact; and my guess is that he would have been both astonished and incredulous had anyone told him that, at the very moment he was writing, certain misguided individuals in that faraway land of

---

[1] Tomaso Garzoni, *La Piazza universale di tutte le professioni del mondo,* discorso CXXV; first ed., Venice, 1585.

heretics were undertaking not only to print books but to print them in the Italian language. He would have wondered, no doubt, what new idiocy had besotted his fellowmen. Certainly he would have considered the perpetrators of this newest folly prime candidates for vacant cells in his projected *Hospital of Incurable Fools*. But we, I think, must view them in quite a different light: first, because some of the works they printed are intrinsically valuable and interesting as art; and second, because these printers and their activities represent a striking phenomenon at a significant moment in the history of British culture. Careless about corrections they undoubtedly were, as Garzoni charges, and all too frequently they expended undue effort on trifles. Still, their total performance was such as to entitle them to be considered at least on a par with those numerous estimable solid citizens, their contemporaries, who busied themselves, for the greater glory of England, with the translation of Italian and other foreign works into the mother tongue.[2]

The questions that naturally arise when we turn to the serious consideration of the printing of Italian books in England between 1550 and 1700 are chiefly these: Who were the printers involved, how were they equipped, how did they proceed, and what was the quality of their product? What kinds of materials did they print, which Italian authors, which particular works? What reasons had they for printing, and what audience did they reach—or hope to reach? What trends are discernible, early and late? Within the compass of a single lecture on so intricate a subject one may, I trust, be allowed the liberty of certain omissions, foreshortenings, and special emphases. At any rate, in the remarks that follow I propose to offer, dispersedly, some tentative answers to these and related questions.[3]

---

[2] For the activities of these worthies, see, especially, M. A. Scott, *Elizabethan Translations from the Italian* (1916); Lewis Einstein, *The Italian Renaissance in England* (1902); F. O. Matthiessen, *Translation, an Elizabethan Art* (1931); Alfred H. Upham, *The French Influence in English Literature* (1908); C. H. Conley, *The First English Translators of the Classics* (1927).

[3] The answers, I hasten to add, are not all my own. In the prepara-

i

By way of getting before us, as it were, the *dramatis personae* (though not in the order of their first appearance), it will be advantageous to name at once some of the more outstanding printers and publishers involved: John Charlewood, Thomas Vautrollier, John Wolfe, Joseph Barnes, John Bill, George Wells. To these may be added the names of several Italians resident in England, most of whom had some connection with one or more of those just listed: John (or Giovanni) Florio, Petruccio Ubaldini, Giacopo Castelvetro, Marc' Antonio de Dominis, and Giovanni Torriano. The joint efforts of these men and of others like them brought from the presses of England between 1550 and 1700 a variegated production of Italian texts in divinity,[4] education, philology, history, philosophy, government propaganda,[5] and—even—of *belles lettres*. To speak of some of these books as being printed in Italian—the grammars, language manuals,

tion of this lecture I have had much valuable aid (and occasional confirmation) from many previous investigators of some phase of my topic. Extremely important among these have been the probing studies of Harry Sellers, "Italian Books Printed in England before 1640," *The Library*, 4th ser., V (1924), 105-128; Frances A. Yates, "Paolo Sarpi's *History of the Council of Trent*," *Journal of the Warburg and Courtauld Institutes*, VII (1944), 123-143; Eleanor Rosenberg, "Giacopo Castelvetro, Italian Publisher in Elizabethan London and His Patrons," *Huntington Library Quarterly*, VI (1943), 119-148; and the late R. C. Simonini, *Italian Scholarship in Renaissance England* (Chapel Hill, 1952).

[4] Under this heading, I suppose, are to be listed G. B. Agnello's *Espositione sopra un libro intitolato apocalypsis spiritus secreti* (1566: STC 199), which I have not seen; M. Florio's *Cathechismo*, Acontius' *Essortatione*, and De Dominis' *Predica*, noticed below; and the *Salmi di David* (1644), printed by "M. F. per Rodolfo Rounthwaite" (Wing, B2760).

[5] I list under this heading without further notice:

1) [William Cecil, Lord Burghley], *Atto della Giustitia d'Inghilterra, esseguito, per la conservatione della commune & christiana pace* (1584: STC 4907), the Italian version of *The Execution of Justice in England* (1583), possibly prepared by Petruccio Ubaldini;

2) *Dichiaratione delle Caggioni*, etc. (1585: STC 9193);

3) *Dichiaratione delle cause*, etc. (1596: STC 9207); and

4) James Butler, Duke of Ormonde, *L'Oratione* . . . "Stampata in Dublino, per Giov. Crooke" (1664: Wing, O454).

5

and dictionaries, for example—is obviously an exaggeration, though the commonly employed device of printing English and Italian in parallel columns or on facing pages did present solid blocks of Italian text and thus provided the printer with all the problems he would have faced had he been printing Italian only. But one follows the rivers before coming to the Ocean Sea.

Conveniently, the year 1550 marked the appearance of a notable book, William Thomas' *Principal Rules of the Italian Grammer, with a Dictionarie for the better understanding of Boccace, Petrarcha, and Dante.* The colophon indicates that it was printed by Thomas Berthelet; successive sixteenth-century editions of 1562 and 1567 were printed by Thomas Powell and by Thomas Wykes. In all these editions Italian words and phrases are printed in a neat and pretty italic type, the English in black letter, with new settings of type for the later editions. The use of brackets of varying sizes in the "grammer" section to encompass the paradigms and other groupings unfortunately gives the pages a chopped-up look repeated in some of the later works for which this first of Italian grammars for Englishmen was an obvious model. The second and much longer part of the volume, the "Dictionarie," though containing approximately 9000 words, is hardly more than a word list—a mere hint of Florio's and Torriano's which were to follow. Thomas, who had traveled extensively in Italy, wrote the work to encourage a friend's Italian studies. It did much more, for it provided the initial formal impulse to that interest in and study of Italian language and literature which was to characterize Englishmen, increasingly, for the next century or more.[6]

We must not linger over the grammars that succeeded

---

[6] For a brief life of Thomas, see E. R. Adair, "William Thomas: A Forgotten Clerk of the Privy Council," in *Tudor Studies* (London, 1924), pp. 133-160; for more information about the *Grammer,* see R. C. Simonini, *Italian Scholarship in Renaissance England,* pp. 42-45; for Thomas' place in the culture of his time, see G. B. Parks, ed., *The History of Italy* (1549) *by William Thomas* (Ithaca, 1963), Introduction.

Thomas'—Henry Granthan's translation (from Latin) of Scipio Lentulo's *Grammatica,* a full and orderly work of which Thomas Vautrollier, an endenizened Huguenot refugee, printed three attractive editions (1574, 1575, 1587); Florio's briefer manuals in his *Firste Fruites* (1578) and *Queen Anna's New World of Words* (1611); John Sandford's *A Grammer or Introduction to the Italian Tongue* (1605); or the much later *True Idiome of the Italian Tongue* (1660), by Peter Paravicino, and *Della Lingua Toscana-Romana* (1657) of the vastly productive language-teacher, Giovanni Torriano, chief bulwark of English Italianists in the second half of the seventeenth century. A word or two might be added concerning Sandford's *Grammer,* printed by Joseph Barnes at Oxford. This is a perfunctory and overpretentious pamphlet of forty-four pages, obviously derived from other grammars and of small utility to anyone needing a practical introduction to the Italian language.[7] Its distinctiveness for us lies in the circumstance of its being, possibly, the crudest piece of printing involving Italian text within our period. Barnes, a bookseller who, on the one hand, since 1584 had been a printer to the University, was also, on the other hand, a licensed vintner;[8] from the appearance of this wretched specimen of printing, a disgrace to any university press, it would seem that he or his workmen had failed to observe the biblical injunction about not letting the one hand know what the other was doing. We shall return to Barnes later in another connection.

Of related pedagogic intent but of rather higher typographic and literary interest is the series of language manuals or conversation-books which begins with Florio's *Firste Fruites* (1578) and extends to Torriano's *Fabrica nova di dialoghi italiani* (1662). Generally speaking, these are cast either in the form of dialogues or of set discourses upon a va-

---

[7] A more favorable estimate of Sandford's book is given in Simonini's *Italian Scholarship in Renaissance England,* pp. 68-71.

[8] R. B. McKerrow, *et al., A Dictionary of Printers and Booksellers in England, Scotland and Ireland, and of Foreign Printers of English Books 1557-1640* (London, 1910), pp. 22-23.

riety of topics which will permit a wide range of vocabulary. If the text is in the form of a discourse, the printing practice usually calls for English and Italian on facing pages; if the form is that of dialogue or of nonsequential phrases, the normal procedure calls for the use of parallel columns. In either case the most commonly followed practice is to print the English text in roman type, the Italian—appropriately—in italic.[9] In certain polyglot texts involving the use of three or more languages, the English may be set in black-letter.[10]

Besides Florio and Torriano, who are not represented by these two titles only, the series includes such books as the *Campo di fior* (1583) and *The Italian Schoole-maister* ([1575], 1597, 1608) of Claude de Sainliens (or Claudius Holyband, *Anglicè*); *Il Passagiere* (1612) by the obscure Benvenuto Italiano, "idiomista in Londra"; and Noel Barlement's *New Dialogues or Colloquies* (1639), which contains also "a little Dictionary of eight Languages": Latin, French, Flemish, German, Spanish, Italian, English, and Portuguese. The author was a Fleming, and the work was first printed abroad; its English printing was by "E.G." (probably Edward Griffin, II) for Michael Sparke, Jr. It was apparently set up without revision directly from a foreign copy, for the dictionary is keyed to the Flemish alphabetical entries, the English is often unidiomatic, and a former owner or reader, presumably English, of the copy I use[11] has corrected in ink the rather plentiful errors in the Italian.

[9]A curious exception to this practice occurs in the *Dialoghi* of Torriano's *Piazza Universale* (1666), where the Italian text is set in roman, the English in italics.

[10]See, for instance, Wolfe's *The Courtier of Count Baldesar Castilio* (1588), where the Italian is printed in italics, the French in roman, the English in black-letter; and the Ponsonby-published *Two Discourses of Master Frances Guiciardin* (1595). This latter may have been printed by Peter Short, apparently at this time proprietor of the device used on the title page; see R. B. McKerrow, *Printer & Publishers' Devices in England and Scotland 1485-1640* (London, 1913), No. 118.

[11]Folger Library: *STC* 1432. The blank verso of the first title page carries signatures of previous owners: "Richard Boys his booke 1642," repeated with date of 1674 and followed by "Josias Tayler His Book," undated.

A subdivision within the series, no less didactic in intention, is devoted to collection of Italian proverbs, sometimes with and sometimes without English equivalents. The earliest of these, entitled *Proverbi vulgari,* appears as the second part of Charles Merbury's *A Briefe Discourse of Royall Monarchie* (1581), a work dedicated by its young author to Queen Elizabeth. No doubt that strongheaded monarch found the politics agreeable and was lightly flattered by the recognition of her proficiency in the Italian tongue. The dedicatory epistle is in Italian, the text of the *Briefe Discourse* in English; the *Proverbi vulgari* section is entirely in Italian except for some marginalia in English.[12] Merbury's interesting collection, possibly (as he claims)[13] less bookish than others, was followed in 1591 by *Florio's Second Frutes . . . to which is annexed his Gardine of Recreation yeelding six thousand Italian Proverbs,* printed by Thomas Orwin (?) for Thomas Woodcock. This, like Merbury's book, is divided into two quite distinct parts, each with its own title page, separate numbering, and discontinuous signatures. Part II, under the title *Giardino di ricreatione,* is entirely in Italian and has one hundred and fifty more than the six thousand proverbs promised on the English title page. This part was apparently also issued separately.[14]

Later collections of Italian proverbs are Torriano's *Select Italian Proverbs* (1642), N. R.'s *Proverbs*—English, French, Dutch, Italian, and Spanish (1659), Peter Paravicino's *Choice Proverbs* (1660), James Howell's *Lexicon Tetraglotton* (1660);[15] and, likewise in the same year as "His Majes-

---

[12]These proverbs have been given a modern edition, with valuable comment, by Charles Speroni, *Proverbi vulgari,* University of California Publications in Modern Philology, vol. 28, no. 3 (Berkeley, 1946).

[13]I have elsewhere indicated my doubts about this; see *Stefano Guazzo and the English Renaissance, 1575-1675* (Chapel Hill, 1961), pp. 123-127.

[14]See *STC* 11100.

[15]The dictionary, which resembles Minsheu, is for our purposes of less interest than the *Paroimiographia, or, Old Sayed Sawes & Adages* which is annexed. This contains proverbs, separately grouped, in English, French, Italian, and Spanish; with the original and the transla-

ty's happy return," Torriano's Gargantuan collection with the interminable title: *Piazza Universale di Proverbi Italiani: Or, A Common Place of Italian Proverbs and Proverbial Phrases. Digested in Alphabetical Order by way of Dictionary. Interpreted, and occasionally Illustrated with Notes. Together with a Supplement of Italian Dialogues. Composed by Gio. Torriano, an Italian, and Professor of that Tongue.* Dedicated to King Charles himself and to the members of the Royal Society, with a separate epistle "Al Lettore Italiano," who, reversing the general pattern of these bilingual publications, will thus be given the means "da poter imparare la Lingua *Inglese*," Torriano's painstaking compilation extends to 338 folio pages in the proverb section proper and contains over ten thousand entries. The work is printed in parallel columns, with the Italian at the left, the English translation (or equivalent) at the right, and with explanatory notes at the end of each letter of the alphabet. This is followed by a "Second Alphabet Consisting of Proverbial Phrases" which are "digested in Alphabetical Order" and which add another 242 pages. Finally, the volume contains the promised *Supplimento di Dialoghi Italiani,* which are described as "non più stampati"—even though the separate title page carries the imprint "London, Printed by *Alice Warren,* For the Author *Anno Dom.* 1662." Altogether, this monumental oak of a tome represents a spectacular growth from the humble duodecimo acorn—the *Select Italian Proverbs*—of nearly a quarter of a century earlier.[16]

Florio's language manuals have been so often discussed

---

tions in parallel columns. The Italian proverbs incorporate most of those (with their translations) found in Torriano's *Select Italian Proverbs.* A collective title page for this part of the volume is dated 1659.

[16]*Select Italian Proverbs; The most significant, very usefull for Travellers, and such as desire that Language* . . . (Cambridge, Roger Daniel, 1642). This tiny 100-page alphabetically arranged volume, departing from the parallel-column form, prints each Italian proverb in italics and follows it by an English translation (with occasional explanatory note) in roman. Daniel published a second edition, in 24°, in 1649, as well as Torriano's *New and Easie Directions* in editions of 1640? (*STC* 24139) and 1645? (Wing, T1926).

and are so readily available[17] that, to conclude this already overlong inspection of such books, we may more profitably limit further consideration of the type to Torriano's less publicized. *Dialoghi.* The dialogues in the *Piazza Universale* were by no means Torriano's first. He had, in fact, included nine dialogues in *The Italian Tutor* (1640),[18] and had published a fuller collection of thirty-seven "occupational" or "occasional" dialogues in his *Della Lingua Toscana-Romana* (1657).[19] These same thirty-seven dialogues were reprinted in 1673 in Torriano's *The Italian Reviv'd* under circumstances and for reasons which he may best be allowed to explain in his own words:

> Had not the late dismal Fire destroyed all the Printed Books which concern the Italian, as to Grammer or Dictionary, (the Book-Trade in General having suffered irreparable loss, above any other whatsoever,) and I my self in particular being involved in the same Fate, as it is well known to many, made a considerable sufferer; there would have been no need for one while of more Books of that nature; but for want of them, the Italian declining, and almost expiring, I thought it necessary to revive it in time, by Reprinting the *Intro-*

---

[17]See, for instance, Frances A. Yates, *John Florio; the Life of an Italian in Shakespeare's England* (Cambridge [Eng.], 1934;); Arundell del Re, ed., Florio's *Firste Fruites* (Taihoku Univ., Formosa, 1936); Silvio Policardi, *John Florio e le relazioni culturali Anglo-Italiane agli albori del XVII secolo* (Montuoro, 1947), pp. 7-99; R. C. Simonini, *Italian Scholarship in Renaissance England*, pp. 55-68, and the same scholar's facsimile reproduction of Florio's *Second frutes* (Gainesville, Fla., 1953). For a slightly different perspective, see Giuliano Pellegrini, *John Florio e il Basilicon Doron di James VI* (Milano, 1961), Introduzione.

[18]*The Italian Tutor, Or a New and Most Compleat Italian Grammer*, London, "Printed by *Tho. Payne*, and . . . sold by *H. Robinson.*" Italian text in italics, English in roman, and printed on facing pages. The title page describes the dialogues as being "made up of Italianismes or neicities of the Language, with the English to them."

[19]*Della Lingua Toscana-Romana. Or, an Introduction to the Italian Tongue. Containing . . . also A new Store House of proper and choice Dialogues most useful for such as desire the speaking part, and intend to travel in Italy, or the Levant.* Italian text in italics, English in roman.

11

duction to the Italian Tongue, that is the Abbridgment of my Introduction in Octavo 1657. affixt to the last Edition of Resolute *John Florio's* Dictionary, corrected, revised, and reverst by me 1659. The English before the Italian, not being in the former Editions.[20]

The grammar is followed by "An Appendix of some few choice Italian Proverbs," numbering 234 (a pathetic shrinkage from the *Piazza*), after which come the *Dialogues,* with separate title page but continuous numbering. More importantly, this first part of the volume (352 pages) is followed by a second part, again with separate title page but with independent pagination and signatures,[21] the *Mescolanza Dolce di varie Historiette,*[22] with the addition of nine *other* dialogues "non più stampati." The total number of dialogues in *The Italian Reviv'd* is, then, forty-six—no small supply of what Shakespeare's Fluellen might have called "tiddle taddle" or "pibble pabble."

But Torriano was to outdialogue himself in his *Fabrica nova di Dialoghi Italiani,* "made suitable to the Apprehension and Imitation of Persons of any Degree or Nation whatsoever, affecting the Italian Tongue, chiefly the English" (title page). Here, indeed, is God's plenty—or the Devil's. For Torriano provides in 115 double-columned folio pages fifty-two fresh dialogues, one for every week of the year. That he was sufficiently impressed with the quantity and quality of his performance may be gathered from his prefatory remarks "To the Reader," which thus begin:

> Having publish'd of late Years, a set of *Italian Dialogues,* in such a Method and Style, as never was done before by any, and since having been mov'd by several Persons of Quality to proceed in the making of more Dialogues of the same Nature and as it were

[20] *The Italian Reviv'd,* "The Preface to the Reader," sig. A2.

[21] A fact which has led to its being considered, erroneously, a discrete publication; see Wing, T1923. Its identity as part of *The Italian Reviv'd* is clearly indicated by Torriano in the preface (sig. A2 verso) to that work.

[22] "Londra, Appresso *Tomaso Roycroft,* ad istanza di Giovanni Martino,"̣ 1673.

cast in the same Mould; To comply with their desires, I have accordingly studied and compos'd a new Set, or Fabrick, as I may term it, of *Italian Dialogues,* both of different Subjects, Matter and Phrase, all along from the former, and exceeding in Number, though sometimes with the same kind of Persons.[23]

The tenor of these remarks is preserved to the end of the preface, even intensified:

> To conclude; there may be Dialogues extant, as namely, *Florio's* First and Second Fruits, *Benvenuto's, Passenger,* large Books both, and others which may contain in them Discourses of a greater Reach, as to a more florid and polite Learning, but if judiciously, and impartially compar'd, none I presume of more ready use, and practice, and that have the knack of the Language, which is all in all, than those lately, and these now published by thy
>
> Gio. Torriano.[24]

Even better than the proverbs that constitute the larger part of this volume, these *Dialoghi* reflect the Garzonian impulse behind Torriano's choice of title; for Garzoni had called his book *Piazza universale di tutte le professioni del mondo.* Torriano's plan is to bring his *Forastiero,* or tourist-learner of Italian, into contact with the representatives of many different professions and social levels, of which the following are but a sample: an accountant, an antiquary, an architect, a barber, a cardinal, a comedian, a cook, a fencing-master, a language-master, a laundress, a merchant, a monk, a physician, a porter, a shoemaker, a tavern-keeper, "a Vizarded Person in Shrovetide." The pattern repeats that of earlier "occupational" dialogues, his own and those of others. No doubt it was an effective practical means of securing that *copia* of vocabulary which would ease the *Forastiero's* way in Italy or usher him safely through Italian conversations and Italian books at home.[25]

---

[23]Sig. a2 recto.

[24]Sig. ¶[1] recto.

[25]For Torriano's effectiveness as a language teacher, see Simonini, *Italian Scholarship in Renaissance England,* pp. 74-80.

13

ii

Having noticed some of the "rude mechanical" and peripherally relevant texts, we may now proceed to the examination of others in which the interest is of a different order.

The distinction of being the first book to be printed entirely in Italian in London (which, in effect, means England) is a disputed honor. A case has been argued for the undated *Cathechismo, cioè forma breve per amaestrare i fanciulli,* printed by Stephen Mierdman,[26] a translation from Cranmer's Latin by Michelangelo Florio, the father of Giovanni, and preacher, in 1550, to the Italian church in London. It would thus have been logical for Florio to have prepared such a catechism for the use of the children within his pastoral charge —though he seems to have been a shepherd of dubious morals.[27] After he had left England with his family under the Marian persecution, publication of such a work would have lost much of its point. Another of his works, a "Life" of Lady Jane Grey, published much later and clearly intended for English readers,[28] again in Italian, was published abroad.

Whether or not the claims for Florio's and Mierdman's primacy be well founded, it has been customary to attribute the distinction to a work from the press of John Wolfe, Petruccio Ubaldini's *La Vita di Carlo Magno Imperadore* (1581).[29] In addition to the negative evidence of the absence of clearly established rival claims, this has the positive evidence of a witness in a position to speak with authority,

[26]Sellers, "Italian Books Printed in England before 1640," pp. 105-107. The book may, however, have been printed abroad: Mierdman fled to the Continent upon the accession of Mary. See the entry for Mierdman in E. G. Duff, *A Century of the English Book Trade* (London, 1905).

[27]He was dismissed under charges of "gross immorality"; see Sir Sidney Lee, *DNB*, entry for John Florio. "Turned out for fornication," unmincingly declares John R. Hale, *England and the Italian Renaissance* (London, 1954), p. 16.

[28]*Historia de la vita e de la morte de l'Illustriss. Signora Giovanna Graia* . . . "Stampato appresso Richardo Pittore, ne l'anno di Christo 1607." Richard Pittore [i.e., Painter], also known as Schilders, printed in London and, later, in Middelburg.

[29]Licensed to Wolfe 17 Jan., 1581; see Arber, *Transcript, II,* 177.

14

Ubaldini himself. Reading this account of Charlemagne, he says, you Englishmen may now have

> cagion di rallegrarvi, che l'opere Italiane non men si possono stampare felicemente in Londra, che le si stampino altrove (essendo questa la prima) per studio, & diligenza di Giovanni Wolfio suo cittadino; per la commoditá del quale altre opere potrete haver nella medesima lingua di giorno in giorno, se la stima, che farete di questa sará tale quale si deve aspettar da huomini desiderosi di lunga, & honorata fama. . . .[30]

The claim is repeated with only slight changes of phrasing in the second edition,[31] though there the Italian of the epistle is strangely transfigured by such hispanisms as "di nuevo" and "he servito." Another independent witness to Wolfe's early activity as a printer of Italian books is found in a small composite volume, *Una Essortatione al timor di Dio. Con alcune rime Italiane, novamente messe in luce,* bearing the imprint "In Londra Appresso Giovanni Wolfio, Servitore de l'Ilustrissimo Signor Filippo Sidnei." This is undated. The *Essortatione* is the work of Giacomo Aconzio (or Acontius); the editor (and author of the *rime*) is Giovan Battista Castiglioni, who says, in the dedicatory epistle to Queen Elizabeth, that the *Essortatione* was among papers left to him by Acontius when he died. He would have printed it sooner, he says, except for its brevity; but lately, finding among his papers a *canzone* in praise of the Queen, together with some shorter poems, he has decided to put them all together and publish this "volumetto," "massimamente con l'occasione d'un giovane di questa Cittá venuto di nuovo d'Italia, ov' ha con molta industria appreso l'arte de lo Stampare." Wolfe had, in point of fact, as is known,[32] spent an indeterminate number of years in Italy between 1572 and 1579 studying and exercising the

---

[30]Dedicatory epistle, "A I Nobili, et illustri Signori, et Magnanimi Cavalieri, & altri Gentil'huomini della natione Inghilese," p. 4.

[31][London, R. Field?], 1599; sig. A2 verso.

[32]R. B. McKerrow, *Dictionary of Printers and Booksellers, 1557-1640,* pp. 296-297.

printer's trade. In any case, once he had returned to England and established a press of his own, he quickly became the most important printer of Italian books in London.[33]

If Ubaldini provided Wolfe copy for his first English-printed book in Italian, he also provided him with copy for at least two other publications and may have acted as press corrector for some of Wolfe's Italian books. An engaging figure in his own right,[34] the long-lived Ubaldini between 1545 and 1563 lived partly in Italy, partly in England; from 1563 until his death sometime after the turn of the century he lived in England, supporting himself by teaching Italian and calligraphy, by transcribing and illuminating manuscripts for presentation to various actual or prospective patrons, by writing, and by cadging as he could. Many Ubaldini manuscripts, of his own composition or copies made from other men's works, have been preserved.[35] In addition to the *Vita*

[33]The most useful account of Wolfe as printer is that of Harry R. Hoppe, "John Wolfe, Printer and Publisher, 1579-1601," *The Library*, XIV (1933), 241-289. Hoppe points out (p. 267) that from 1594 none of Wolfe's books were printed by him, but by Adam Islip or John Windet, who took over his presses, types, and ornaments. Three of Wolfe's early-printed Italian books, not discussed below, were

   1) Marco Antonio Pigafetta's *Itinerario* (1585: *STC* 19914); and

   2) Giovanni Battista Aurellio, *Esamine di varii giudicii de i Politici* (1587: *STC* 964). I have not seen either of these.

   3) Francesco Betti, *Lettera di Francesco Betti gentilhuomo Romano, All'Illustriss. & Eccellentiss. S. Marchese di Pescara . . . Stampata la seconda volta* (1589: not in *STC*). The little octavo is creditably printed in a fine italic type. Betti's dedicatory epistle, dated "Il di ultimo d'Agosto 1588. in Basilea," is directed to Horatio Palavicini (or Palavicino), a notable London merchant who was presumably the means of bringing the work to Wolfe's attention.

[34]See the article on him, by J. M. Rigg, in the *DNB;* the thesis by Maria Vera Ricci, *Petruccio Ubaldini: Contributo allo studio dell' influsso della Rinascenza italiana sulla Rinascenza inglese* (Firenze, 1940); and, more fully and authoritatively, the study in Giuliano Pellegrini, *Un fiorentino alla corte d'Inghilterra nel Cinquecento: Petruccio Ubaldini* (Torino, 1967), pp. 7-55. The last volume also prints (pp. 57-152), from manuscript, Ubaldini's *Relazione d'Inghilterra.*

[35]See *DNB,* s.v., and Ricci, *op. cit.,* pp. 101-102. Several choice specimens, as we shall later see, were among the MSS in the library of John, Lord Lumley.

di Carlo Magno, seven other of Ubaldini's Italian writings
were published in England: *Descrittione del Regno di Scotia,
et delle Isole sue adiacenti* (1588), largely translated or
adapted from Hector Boece;[36] *Le Vite delle Donne illustri del
Regno d'Inghilterra* (1591);[37] *Parte Prima delle breve Di-
mostrationi, et precetti utilissimi* (1592); *Lo Stato delle tre
corti* (1594); *Scelta di alcune attioni, et di varii accidenti*
(1595); *Rime* (1596); and *Militia del Gran Duca di Thos-
cana* (1597). Of these seven Wolfe printed the first two; the
others, all without the name of the printer, have been as-
signed to Richard Field upon inconclusive evidence.[38]

Ubaldini, an elegant exotic—"Cittadin Fiorentino" as he
continued to describe himself—was personally known to a
select circle in and around the Court, but his writing could
hardly have commanded much attention elsewhere. What
Wolfe needed, as an enterprising new printer-publisher in an
area not already preempted by others—those "monopolists"
whom he so bitterly fought—was a roster of names of resounding international appeal. These he was quick to seek
out; and one of the first he chose was one who was still in hot
request almost a century later. In the forty-second dialogue
of his *Piazza Universale,* Torriano presents his Stranger in
conversation with a Roman Bookseller:

> "I am seeking the works of A[retino]," says the
> Stranger.
> "You may seek them from one end of the Row to
> the other, and not find them," replies the bookseller.
> "And why?"
> "Because they are forbidden, both the *Postures* [*Fig-
> ure*] and *Discourses* [*Raggionamenti*], that imbracing
> of men and women together in unusual manners, begets
> a scandal, and the Inquisition permits no such matters,

---

[36]Andrew Coventry, ed., *Descrittione del Regno di Scotia* (Edinburgh, 1829), Bannatyne Club reprint, pp. vi-vii.

[37]In the dedicatory epistle to this work, directed to Queen Elizabeth, Ubaldini describes himself (sig. ¶2 verso) as "suo servo gia di
anni xxvii"—i.e., since 1564.

[38]H. Sellers, "Italian Books Printed in England before 1640," pp.
120-122.

17

Il Pastor Fido

TRAGICOMEDIA
PASTORALE

DI BATTISTA GVARINI.

Al Serenifs. D. Carlo Emanuele.
Duca di Sauoia &c, Dedicata.

Nelle Reali Nozze di S. A. con la Serenifs. Infante
D. Caterina d'Auftria.

L O N D R A,

Per Giouanni Volfeo, a fpefe di
Giacopo Cafteluetri, M D X C I.

Title page of a volume printed by John Wolfe, showing his adaptation
of the Giuntine lily device and the Wolfe-Castelvetro publishing
combination. Reproduced by permission from a copy in The Folger
Shakespeare Library.

18

it condemns all such sordid things, nay not so much, but the Amarous Adventures in Romances it condemns."[39]

The first of Wolfe's Aretinesque publications, all printed anonymously or under false imprint, was *La Prima [e seconda] parte de Ragionamenti di M. Pietro Aretino, cognominato il Flagello de Prencipi, il Veritiero, e'l Divino* (1584), an octavo neatly printed in italic type. The volume consists of three parts: the *Ragionamenti*, Parts I and II (sigs. A-Yy6), and two works by Annibale Caro, the *Comento di ser Agresto*[40] and the *Nasea* (sigs. AA-HH3). The first of these last two formed part of a sportive literary wrangle between Caro and Francesco Maria Molza. When it was first published (by Blado of Rome) in 1539, the printer entered into the spirit of the joke and signed himself *Barbagrigia*—"Graybeard." In all his printings of Aretino's works Wolfe took over this ready-made pseudonym, invented transparently fictitious places of publication (Bengodi, Valcerca), and bepistled his readers with amusing accounts of his formerly printed and forthcoming Aretiniana.

After the *Prima parte,* Wolfe's next publication of Aretino was the *Quattro Comedie del Divino Pietro Aretino* (1588), neatly printed in a small roman type. The title page, dated but lacking other indications, has a medallion portrait of Aretino encircled by the legend "D. Petrus Aretinus Flagellum Principum," the same device to be used in the next year on the title page of Part III of the *Ragionamenti*. The four comedies, each with its separate title page, are *Il Marescalco, La Cortegiana, La Talanta,* and *L'Hipocrito.* At the end of the volume Wolfe prints five (!) pages of "errori scorsi nella stampa," which is his own distinctive heading for his lists of errata.[41] This unusually long list of faults escaped is followed,

---

[39]*Piazza Universale; Dialoghi,* p. 80.

[40]*Agretso,* as Wolfe misprints it.

[41]It so appears, for instance, in the Guarini-Tasso *Pastor Fido . . . Aminta* (1591), in the Machiavelli *Prencipe* (1584), *Asino d'Oro* (1588)—where the list of errors is somewhat optimisti-

on the verso of the final leaf, by some remarks of "Il Corret-tore al benigno Lettore," in which he explains that the great number of errors has been occasioned by his not having had in hand until very late in the printing correct copies of the texts he was reproducing. There may be something more than fiction in the assertion.

The third and last of Wolfe's Aretines is *La Terza, et ultima parte de Ragionamenti del Divino Pietro Aretino* (1589). In a prefatory epistle, "Lo stampatore ai Lettori," Wolfe pretends (or, it may be, asserts veraciously) that the clamor of his readers for the Third Part of the *Ragionamenti*—"promessavi (s'io non erro) dal valente Barbagrigia l'anno di salute M.D.LXXXIIII. quand egli stampò la Primiera, e la Secōda parte de gli altri Ragionamenti di questo Auttore"—has led him, diverting him from his plans to print others of Aretino's works, to issue the present book.

Wolfe's other Worthies, in addition to Aretino, included an Italian version of the *Agricola* of Tacitus,[42] a thin quarto of forty-eight pages well printed in a firm medium-sized italic type and possibly the handsomest of Wolfe's Italian productions; a trilingual version of Castiglione's *Courtier* (1588); Guarini's *Pastor fido* and Tasso's *Aminta*, issued together in one volume in 1591; and assorted works of Machiavelli. And the greatest of these was, of course, the last.

Machiavelli's works, placed on the *Index* in 1559 and rigorously suppressed in Italy, were there and elsewhere in great demand.[43] No English translation of his major work, *Il Principe*, was published in England before 1640, though several translations are known to have circulated in manuscript in

cally limited to fifteen—and *Arte della Guerra* (1587), and in the Aretino *Terza, et ultima parte de Ragionamenti* (1589).

[42] *La Vita di Giulio Agricola scritta sincerissimamente. da Cornelio Tacito suo Genero. et Messa in volgare da Giovan. Maria Manelli.* Londra, nella Stamperia di Giovanni Wolfio, 1585.

[43] On the suppression of Machiavelli's writings, consequent scarcity of *bona fide* Italian-printed editions, and flourishing publication under false imprints, see Salvatore Bongi's *Annali di Gabriel Giolito de' Ferrari da Trino di Monferrato Stampatore in Venezia* (Roma, 1890-95), 2 vols., II (1895), 415-418.

Elizabethan England.[44] Here, clearly, was a sure-fire seller. Statists from polypragmatic Gabrielissimo Harvey to the very heads of government[45] would avidly purchase Machiavelli, in translation or in the original. Wolfe knew when he had come upon a good thing. So the publishing began: *Il Principe* and the *Discorsi,* separate volumes with "alcune altre operette" thrown in for good measure, appeared in the same year, both with the false imprint, "In Palermo, appresso gli heredi d'Antoniello degli Antonielli, a xxviii di Gennaio, 1584." With the list of errata in *Il Principe,* Wolfe directs a note to "L'aveduto & discreto lettore," asking him to correct minor errors and to pardon the "compositori, a quali, per esser eglino Siciliani, & per non sapere la favella toscana, con tutta la loro diligenza, non gli hanno potuti schifare." The "Sicilians" he is talking about are of course English, and what he is saying is that, under the restrictive regulations of the Stationers' Company concerning the employment of aliens, English printers cannot employ journeymen capable of handling the Italian language. The complaint is not Wolfe's alone, nor is it limited to this early period.[46] William Aglionby, translator of the pseudo-Sarpian *Opinion of Padre Paolo,* could write in 1689:

[44] G. N. G. Orsini, *Studii sul Rinascimento italiano in Inghilterra* (Firenze, 1937), pp. 1-19; Hardin Craig, ed., *Machiavelli's The Prince, an Elizabethan Translation* (Chapel Hill, 1944), pp. xiii-xxxii.

[45] As a matter of record, Lord Burghley's books, when auctioned in 1687, were found to have among them copies of Wolfe's edition of the *Discorsi* and *Principe* ("Palermo," 1584), and the non-Wolfian *Historie di Nich. Machiavelli* (Vinegia, 1554). His library, whether they were added by himself or by his heirs, also contained Wolfe's printings of Ubaldini's *Descrittione del Regno di Scotia* (1588) and *Vite delle Donne Illustri d'Inghilterra* (1581), as well as two Wolfe-printed Aretinos, the *Ragionamenti* (1584) and *Quattro Comedie* (1588). See *Bibliotheca Illustris.: sive Catalogus* . . . 1587 (= Wing *STC* B5726).

[46] See Benvenuto Italiano, *Il Passagiere* (1612): ". . . the *Printer* (notwithstanding otherwise, hee is no lesse a discreete then an honest man) being but a stranger in the Italian Tongue, in the Copie he was much troubled" (sig. A6); and John Florio, *Firste Fruites,* after errata list: "Cortese Lettore . . . vogli scusar il [*sic*] Stampatore, perche lui non sa ne parlar, ne intender Italiano, e percio merita perdono."

> I have no more to say, but that this is a very faithful Translation from an Original Manuscript communicated to me in Italy, where it begins to creep abroad; and if we had in *England* the conveniency of Workmen that could Print *Italian* correctly, I would have publish'd both the Original and my Translation together.[47]

However hampered he may have been by his "Sicilians," Wolfe continued to print Machiavelli, issuing in 1587 both the *Historie di Nicolo Machiavelli, Cittadino et secretario Fiorentino,* with its bold falsification of imprint, "In Piacenza appresso gli heredi di Gabriel Giolito de Ferrari,"[48] and *I Sette libri dell'arte della guerra.* The latter, we might observe, had appeared in English translation a quarter of a century earlier, and the translated *Florentine History* was to be published in 1595. The *Arte della guerra* prints another long list of "Errori scorsi nella stampa,"[49] "avvertendo che si sono notati solamente i piu importanti," and noting that errors in pagination, "sendocene errati assai," are also omitted. Both notations are understatements. In the *Historie* volume the epistle "al benigno lettore" promises the speedy supplying of other works of "questo nobile scrittore . . . che sono le sue Comedie, le sue Novelle il suo Asino d'oro, alcuni suoi Capitoli, e'l suo Decinale compendio delle cose fatte in dieci anni in Italia."[50] This judicious whetting of his readers' appetite Wolfe followed up the next year with his publication of *Lasino doro di Nicolo Macchiavelli, con tutte laltre sue operette.*[51] With this volume Wolfe completes his Machiavelli,

---

[47]*The Opinion of Padre Paolo . . . In what manner the Republick of Venice ought to govern themselves . . . to have perpetual Dominion* (London, 1689), sig. A12 recto-verso.

[48]For the identification of Wolfe as the printer of these works of Machiavelli, and for other interesting particulars concerning him, see Salvatore Bongi, *Annali di Gabriel Giolito,* II (1895), 419 ff.

[49]Sig. T6.

[50]Sig. A6 verso.

[51]With false imprint, "In Roma 1588." The other *operette* are four *capitoli* ("Occasione," "Fortuna," "Ingratitudine," "Ambitione"), the *Decinale compendio,* the novella *Belphagor,* and two comedies, *La Mandragola* and *La Clizia.*

though he declares[52] that he would gladly print more were more available to him.

Two further titles among Wolfe's Italian books are of special interest. One is the previously mentioned composite volume of Guarini-Tasso, the *Pastor fido* and the *Aminta,* a work which puts between the same covers the two most popular pastoral dramas of the age and, significantly, carries the imprint "Londra, per Giovanni Volfeo, a spese di Giacopo Castelvetri, 1591"; the other is Juan Gonzalez de Mendoza's *L'historia del gran regno della China, fatta vulgare da F. Avanzi,* which, though bearing the false imprint "in Vinegia, per Andrea Muschio, 1587," is known both to have been printed by Wolfe and to have been sponsored by Castelvetro.[53] The precise relationship between these two men is obscure, but there is a distinct possibility that Castelvetro may in some way have assisted Wolfe in the editing or printing of his Italian publications.

Aside from the Wolfian books the only other significant block of Italian books from an Elizabethan press is the group of six works by the famous Giordano Bruno, all published during or immediately following his stormy visit to Oxford University, 1583–1585. All except one, which is merely dated 1584, bear false imprints of Venice or Paris, though (to quote the prime authority on the matter) "it has been always admitted that these books were English printed."[54] Thomas Vautrollier was at one time thought to have printed them; but that attribution has proved groundless. To quote our authority again, "all the books are from the same font of type and have the same initials and head-ornaments,"[55] and their printer has now been conclusively identified as John Charlewood. I do not propose to discuss these books

---

[52]Prefatory epistle, sig. A2 verso.

[53]See Eleanor Rosenberg, "Giacopo Castelvetro Italian Publisher in Elizabethan London and His Patrons," *Huntington Library Quarterly,* VI, no. 2 (1943), 119-148.

[54]Harry Sellers, "Italian Books Printed in England before 1640," p. 123. For further discussion of the identity of the printer, I once again refer the reader to this invaluable and often-cited article.

[55]*Ibid.*

further, but will simply list their titles here for convenient reference on a later occasion: *La Cena de le Ceneri* (1584), *De la causa, principio, et Uno* (1584), *De l'infinito universo et Mondi* (1584), *Spaccio de la Bestia Trionfante* (1584), *De gl'Heroici Furori* (1585), and *Cabala del Cavallo Pegaseo* (1585).

A cursory glance is likewise all that can be spared for a scattering of certain other works from various presses: Richard Carew's translation of the first five cantos of Tasso's *Godfrey of Bulloigne, or the Recoverie of Hierusalem* (1594), printed by John Windet, with English and Italian on facing pages—a handsomely printed volume, fully as attractive as any contemporaneous Italian printings of either version of Tasso's famous poem (and rather better than most of those appearing in the 'nineties); Thomas Morley's *Primo libro delle ballette a cinque voci* (1595), printed by Thomas East, which, with the music of the "Cantus" gives the Italian text of twenty-one songs; *Two Discourses of Master Frances Guiciardin* (1595), which reprints the Basel 1561 edition in Italian, Latin, and French, adding to these an English translation of certain parts omitted from the regular printings of Guicciardini's *Historia d'Italia;* Antimo Galli's *Rime . . . all'Illustrissima Signora Elizabetta Talbot-Grey* (1609), printed at the Eliot's Court press by Melchisidec Bradwood, a book of fashionable complimentary and laudatory poems, among the latter, one—a sonnet[56]—addressed to Giovanni Florio; and, finally, Lodovico Petrucci's *Raccolta d'alcune rime* (1613). This last, with Italian and Latin texts on facing pages, was a product of Joseph Barnes's Oxford press—largely, one may suppose, because its self-pitying author happened at that particular moment of his misadventures to be resident in Oxford.[57] The printing of the Italian part is extrav-

---

[56]Sig. D2.

[57]Omitted from discussion here is another rare "literary" work which I have not seen, Francesco Peretto's *Gli Occhi. Oda. All'Illustrissima Contessa Lucia Bedford. Con altri vari componimenti heroici regii* (1616: STC 19624). "In Londra, presso G. Purslow." The *STC* lists only the copy in Lincoln Cathedral.

Portrait of Lodovico Petrucci, from his *Apologia* (1619). Reproduced by permission from a copy in The Folger Shakespeare Library.

agantly inaccurate,[58] the Latin a little better. Lodovico Petrucci is sometimes said to have been the son of Petruccio Ubaldini, who *does* seem to have had a son named Lodovico. But, as Shakespeare says, this is not the man.[59]

iii

Bypassing, for the time being, the highly important dictionaries of Florio and Torriano, we come now to consider a final group of Italian books all from a single press, that of John Bill, King's Printer. Bill, whose early activities were rather those of purchasing agent and bookseller than those of printer, was in Italy in 1602–1603 supplying books for Sir Thomas Bodley.[60] He is known also to have supplied Italian books to the ninth Earl of Northumberland, "the Wizard Earl."[61] He may, thus, have had a special interest in Italian books;[62] but it is much more likely that his first piece of Italian printing, one of those nauseously plentiful seventeenth-century productions described on their title pages as ". . . a

[58]Sig. Q2, in a full page of forty-three lines, records "I principali errori, commessi nell'Italiano di questo libro." The Latin errata require only seven lines.

[59]An account of Petrucci and his various "persecutioni," including his final imprisonment in the Fleet, has been published by Vittorio Gabrieli in *English Miscellany*, XI (1960), 287-315, with appendices (pp. 316-332) containing selections from his poems. The article also reproduces a contemporary portrait of Petrucci.

[60]See G. W. Wheeler, ed., *Letters of Sir Thomas Bodley to Thomas James* (Oxford, 1926), pp. 65, 76, 79. A letter from London, dated Feb. 18, [1603], indicates that Bodley hopes "to be provided, by Io. Billes diligence . . . For he hath bin already, at Venice, Ferrara, Padua, Verona, Brescia, Mantua, Pavia, Milan, Florence, Pisa, Rome &c. and hath bought as many bookes, as he knewe I had not, amounting to the summe, of at the lest, 400 li. besides those that he may have bought sins his last unto me, which was in December."

[61]Historical MSS Comm., Appdx. to Sixth Report (1877), p. 231, col. 1.

[62]This assumption is only very slenderly supported, if at all, by the presence of Italian books—Spanish are more plentiful—in a catalogue of sequestered goods which presumably contained a combination, left to his son, of his library and unsold stock; see J. L. Lievsay and R. B. Davis, "A Cavalier Library, 1643," University of Virginia *Studies in Bibliography*, VI (1954), 141-160.

Sermon preach't," came his way by virtue of his being King's Printer—a command performance, in short. This was a certain unremarkable *Predica fatta la prima Domenica dell'- avvento quest anno 1617 in Londra,* delivered before the Italian congregation in the Mercers' chapel, by a rather remarkable man, Marc' Antonio de Dominis. Three weeks later Bill also published an English translation of the sermon.

De Dominis, a renegade Catholic who had defected from his Archbishopric of Spalato, in Dalmatia, and had made his way in 1616 to England, was something of a nine days' wonder, and was in England under the encouragement and special protection of both the Archbishop of Canterbury and King James himself.[63] He is now probably best remembered, by Englishmen at least, as the meddling editor of Paolo Sarpi's *Historia del Concilio Tridentino* and as the "Fat Bishop" caricatured in Middleton's *Game at Chesse.* In his own time he was renowned as a religious controversialist and as author of the important *De Republica Ecclesiastica.* All his works, whether in Latin, in Italian, or in English, coming from the pen of so eminent a convert to Protestantism, were useful as propaganda for the Establishment—which no doubt accounts for Bill's publication of so many of them.[64]

To the year 1617 also belongs the first issue of a much more important work printed by Bill, an Italian translation of Bacon's *Essays* and his *Wisdom of the Ancients,* under the title *Saggi morali del Signore Francesco Bacone, Cavagliere Inglese. Con un altro Trattato della Sapienza de gli Antichi.*[65] The translation, based upon the 1612 English edition of

---

[63]Particulars concerning his life may be read in Henry Newland, *The Life and Contemporaneous Church History of Antonio de Dominis* (Oxford and London, 1859), laudatory and not wholly dependable; in Logan Pearsall Smith, *The Life and Letters of Sir Henry Wotton* (Oxford, 1907), 2 vols.; and in R. C. Bald, ed., Middleton's *A game at chesse* (Cambridge, Eng., 1929).

[64]See *STC* 6994-7007.

[65]R. W. Gibson, *Francis Bacon: A Bibliography of His Works and of Baconiana to the year 1750* (Oxford, 1950), nos. 33-35. A copy of the 1617 issue is in the Lambeth Palace Library. Gibson also records several Italian-printed editions of this translation, down to 1626.

the *Essays*, is characterized by some curious omissions and phrasings and is clearly intended for a foreign audience, as is indicated by its being dedicated to "Don Cosimo [II] Gran Duca di Toscana."[66] Sir Tobie Mathew, Bacon's friend, who signs the dedication, is sometimes said to have made the translation, but the language of the dedication—admittedly dubious—seems to point in the direction of William Cavendish.[67] This is an extraordinary moment in the history of the printing of Italian texts in England, for it marks the first time that a work of English literature (as distinct from propaganda) had been translated into Italian, printed in England, and exported to an Italy already entering upon an era of cultural eclipse.[68]

Sharing literary honors with the English-printed first editions of Bruno must be named, finally, another Italian work first issued from the press of John Bill: Paolo Sarpi's historical masterpiece, the *History of the Council of Trent*. Its full title, as it appeared in 1619 over the anagrammatic pseudonym of "Pietro Soave Polano" (i.e., Paolo Sarpio Veneto), was *Historia del Concilio Tridentino, nella quale si scoprono tutti gl'artificii della Corte di Roma, per impedire che né la veritá di dogmi si palesasse, né la riforma del Papato, & della Chiesa si tratasse.* This bellicose and tendentious expansion of the author's original title, the simple *Historia del Concilio Tridentino*, as it is preserved in a partially autograph manuscript in the Marciana,[69] was the work of M. A. de Dominis, who edited the work and dedicated it to King James. Because of this editorial connection and be-

---

[66]So, at least, in an issue of 1618.

[67]For Mathew's editing (if not translating) of the work, and for its reception in Italy, see Giuliano Pellegrini, *La prima versione dei "Saggi morali" di Bacone e la sua fortuna* (Firenze, 1942).

[68]I omit from consideration here another Italian work printed by Bill, Alessandro Gatti's *La Caccia* (1619), a book of which I have seen no copy.

[69]Cod. ital., V, 25. The manuscript is in the hand of one of Sarpi's copyists, Fra Marco Fanzano, but has extensive corrections in Sarpi's own hand. See Giovanni Gambarin, ed., *Istoria del Concilio Tridentino* (Bari, 1935), 3 vols., III, 403.

cause of some ambiguous wording in the dedicatory epistle,[70] De Dominis was long thought to have been the Only
Begetter—or at least procurer—of the manuscript; and the
assertion has sometimes been made[71] that he secured his copy
in Venice and either brought it with him or left it in the hands
of the Reverend William Bedell. It is now known, however,
that the manuscript was obtained specifically at the instigation of Archbishop George Abbott, who sent Nathaniel Brent
to Italy with instructions to acquire a copy. Correspondence
between the two men indicates that Brent received the manuscript in installments which he then forwarded dutifully and
cautiously, but safely, to the Archbishop.[72] Both Brent and De
Dominis figure in the subsequent history of Sarpi's book,
Brent as translator of the English version which appeared in
1620 and De Dominis as one of the several men who had a
hand in the Latin translation, also printed in 1620. Bill,
"Regio Stampatore," was also the printer-publisher of both
translations and thus has a threefold connection with this famous book. With his sensational *Historia del Concilio Tridentino*, a stately folio of some 800 pages, seen through the

---

[70]*Historia del Concilio Tridentino,* sig. a3: "Questa sua fatica à me,
& á poichissimi [*sic*] di lui molto confidenti nota, reputai io degna
d'essere guidata alla luce, onde m'affaticai non poco per cavargliene
copia delle mani; & havuta questa preciosa gioia, da lui poco stimata,
non hò giudicato doversi ella piú tener occulta, quantonque io non
sappia quello fusse per sentire esso Autore, ó come havesse ad inter-
pretare questa mia risolution di publicarla."
    "Et io che sono il portatore di questo si preggiato dono, andaró
gioiendo che mi si sia presentata si bella occasione a V.M. che non
solamente con le mie, ma anco con l'altrui fatiche desidero impie-
garmi tutto a servirla" (sig. a3 verso).
[71]See, for instance, Newland, *Life of De Dominis*, p. 109.
[72]The original account of this procedure, long forgotten or ne-
glected, is to be read in Lewis Atterbury, ed., *Some Letters relating to
the History of the Council of Trent* (London, 1705). More recent
elaborations and interpretations of this material are found in Frances
A. Yates, "Paolo Sarpi's *History of the Council of Trent," Journal of
the Warburg and Courtauld Institutes*, VII (1944), 123-143, and in
Gaetano Cozzi, "Fra Paolo Sarpi, l'Anglicanesimo e la *Historia del
Concilio Tridentino," Rivista Storica Italiana*, LXVIII (1956), fasc.
iv, pp. 559-619.

29

press by a competent but misguided[73] editor who was himself almost as great a sensation as the book he introduced, we may appropriately end our rapid survey of English-printed Italian texts.

Glancing back over the terrain we have covered, we now perceive certain larger features of the landscape. Wolfe, Charlewood, and Bill emerge as the most significantly involved printers; Thomas, Ubaldini, Florio, Castelvetro, De Dominis, and Torriano as the most energetic and ardent promoters of printing in Italian. Grammars, language manuals, dictionaries—utilitarian publications—loom large in the first half of our period, diminish in the second, when French language and culture become increasingly influential. From the publishers' point of view, motives of profit and propaganda prompt the selection of works to be printed. And from the consumers' point of view these selections often enough reflect current interest in certain forms—dialogues, proverbs, pastorals—or in individuals to whom some degree of scandal or public notoriety may be said to adhere—Aretino, Bruno, Machiavelli, De Dominis, Sarpi. Curiously, no English printers undertook to provide texts of any of the major authors in whom, a priori, they and their readers might have been supposed to have a legitimate interest: Dante, Petrarch, Boccaccio,[74] Ariosto—writers who, except for Harington's translation of the *Orlando Furioso*, were not even well represented in translation. And translation itself, along with the perduring unavailability of competent workmen, may have had something to do with the noticeable decline, toward the

[73]Besides supplying the inflammatory additions to the title page and the rabid anti-Romanist tenor of the dedication to King James, De Dominis also undertook to "improve" Sarpi's language; see G. Gambarin, ed., *Istoria del Concilio Tridentino,* III, 417-420, and Giovanni Getto, *Paolo Sarpi,* 2nd ed. (Firenze, Olschki, 1967), pp. 333-341.

[74]Under date of 13 Sept., 1587, Wolfe was licensed to print *"Il decamerone di* Boccacio in Italian and *the historie of China* [J. Gonzalez de Mendoza's] both in Italian and English." See Arber, *Transcript,* II, 475. The Gonzalez "both in Italian and English" appeared (see *STC* 12003-04); no trace remains of the Boccaccio.

end of our period, in the number of English-printed Italian texts. For numerous as had been the Elizabethan and Jacobean translations from Italian, that plenty was surpassed by the number produced between 1625 and 1700.

The restitution of a Frenchified Court, the ascendent star of French manners and letters, the greater availability of translations, and the falling attractions of Italy all combined in such a way as to write, by 1700, an effective finis to the movement we have studied.

II

Italian Books on English Shelves

The supply of Italian books in Tudor and Stuart England was not dependent exclusively, or even primarily, on the product of English presses. But after the institution of the *Index librorum prohibitorum* and the drastic curtailment of the book trade in Italy that followed the decrees of the Council of Trent, it did become increasingly difficult for Englishmen to procure the Italian authors and unexpurgated editions they wanted. Secure them they did, however, and it now becomes our pleasant concern to examine their acquisitions. Unfortunately, much of the evidence, along with many of the books, has now perished. We must patch the story together from such records as remain.

What Italian books, precisely—not translations—did Englishmen own and read? Who were their favorite authors and what were their favorite disciplines? How did Italian books compare in numbers with those of other vernaculars on their shelves? What current tastes are reflected in the titles they chose? How were the books acquired, who owned them, and what has been their subsequent fate?

Answers to such questions (and others will present themselves as we proceed) are to be extracted, bit by bit, from a great variety of sources: published and manuscript catalogues of public and private libraries; old wills, letters, and inventories of goods; diaries, journals, and commonplace books; booksellers' catalogues; *ex libris* records; printed acknowledgements of sources used by authors in the preparation of their own books; lists of recommended books for reading; and casual literary allusions. Not all of these, obviously, will be of equal value for our purposes. Some of them may supply

33

only inferential information and must, therefore, be used with caution. Many a man no doubt read Italian books he did not own; and some men read them in places other than England. But when we come upon an Englishman saying, "I have seen," "I have read," "I have had in hand" such-and-such a book—as when Sir John Harington writes[1] to his "Sweet Mall," "Send me up, by my manne Combe, my Petrarche" —we are fairly safe in assuming that the book in question was physically present in England. And it is with such books, and such books only, that we are here dealing.

i

We can do no better than to begin *in medias res* with the "still resolute" John Florio's Italian-English dictionary, *A Worlde of Wordes,* published in 1598.[2] Opposite the first page of the text of his "most copious and exact Dictionarie" Florio has set down "The names of the Bookes and Auctors, that have bin read of purpose, for the accomplishing of this Dictionarie, and out of which it is collected." These number seventy-two, among whom figure Sannazaro, Boccaccio, Aretino, Guazzo, Franco, Speroni, della Casa, Tasso, Garzoni, Castiglione, Doni, Giovio, Caro, Tolomei, Petrarch, Berni, and Botero. The text, incidentally, runs to 462 triple-columned pages and the entries to an estimated 24,000. When Florio republished the work, much altered, as *Queen Anna's New World of Words* (1611), his "brainebabe"[3] had grown

---

[1] Norman E. McClure, ed., *The Letters and Epigrams of Sir John Harington* (Philadelphia, 1930), p. 98.

[2] Folio; printed by Arnold Hatfield for Edward Blount. Blount, it might be noted, was also the publisher of the first edition (1603) of Florio's translation of Montaigne's *Essays.* In the Folger copy (No. 1) of the *Worlde of Wordes* that I have used, Florio has supplied an autograph dedication, in a beautiful flowing hand, "Alla non meno Nobile, generosa, et Illma che gratiosa, virtuosa, et d'ogni honore meritissima S^{ra} e Dama, la S^{ra} Elisabeta Bartley, Giovanni Florio suo sempre assequen^{mo} et affettion^{mo} Servitore di cuore brama, desidera, et augura il colmo d'ogni suo desio, et il godimento di tutte le vere felicità." The printed dedication is to Roger, Earl of Rutland, Henry, Earl of Southampton, and Lucy, Countess of Bedford.

[3] Sig. ¶2 verso.

to something like 90,000 entries, and his list of authorities from 72 to 252.

Inasmuch as this greatly expanded list might well serve as a model for the ideal library of a Jacobean Italianate Englishman, it is worth our further scrutiny. Notable additions to it are Bembo, Bruno, Dante, Giraldi Cinthio, Guicciardini, Guarini, the *Croce racquistata* of Francesco Bracciolini—hot from the press—Tansillo, Pulci, Panigarola, Ariosto, Firenzuola, Luigi Groto, "Tutte L'opere di Nicolo Macchiavelli," and a large number of plays. Florio's choices reflect an intelligent concern for a balance between "classic" and current writers. Among the English-printed Italian books on the list are the *Quattro Comedie dell'Aretino,* Wolfe's printing of 1588, and five of the six works of Bruno printed by Charlewood. And among other recently published works, he includes the *"Bibbia Sacra tradotta da Giovanni Diodati"* (1607), uncle of Milton's Damon. There are also some not unexpected overlappings of titles in this list and that of William Drummond of Hawthornden, which will be examined later.[4] Interestingly, Drummond's list includes Florio's *Worlde of Wordes.*

Since we last saw him, not long ago, in a graceless stance, let us next return in grateful recompense to the Oxford printer-vintner Joseph Barnes. The volume we look at now is dated 1605 and shows the same weary ornaments and capitals, the same fuzzy type, and the same coarse paper that we have seen before. But this time there is a redeeming feature: the author-compiler is Thomas James, first Librarian of the Bodleian, and the volume is the first printed catalogue of that institution.[5] This pudgy quarto of 655 pages offers us an incomparable insight into what, at this remarkable moment in

---

[4] See below, pp. 40-42.

[5] *Catalogus Librorum Bibliothecae Publicae quam Vir Ornatissimus Thomas Bodlaeus Eques Auratus in Academia Oxoniensi nuper instituit . . .* Oxoniae, Apud Iosephum Barnesium. Ann. Dom. 1605. All dates accompanying titles from this catalogue, as well as those from James's second *Catalogus,* below, are the dates of editions listed, not of the original publications.

the nation's history, was considered a suitable supply of Italian books, not merely for a university library, but for what was then the greatest public library in Britain.

The books in James's catalogue are listed in loosely alphabetical order under four general divisions: Theology, Medicine, Law, and Arts. A series of appendices follows the main part of the catalogue and offers additional titles under each head. The total number of titles thus listed I estimate, in round numbers, to be between thirteen and fourteen thousand. Of this number, my running count (for which I offer no guarantee of accuracy) adds up to 509 entries of Italian works—51 in Theology, 27 in Medicine, 3 in Law, and 428 in Arts. Books in Latin, of course, greatly outnumber all others, with the English in a shaky second. The Spanish—surprisingly—and the French perhaps outnumber the Italian books in all divisions except the Arts. And except in this area of humane letters few of the Italian works are of any particular value, though any of them would now fetch an astronomical price if it fell into the hands of a bookseller with a customer like Bodley.

In this final section, of the great names there are present Dante (with commentaries of Velutello, Landino, and Daniello); Petrarch (with commentaries or expositions of Velutello, Gesualdo, Filelfo, and others); Boccaccio, represented by the *Decamerone* (1552) and the *Filocopo* (1551); and Ariosto, represented by both the *Orlando Furioso* (1543) and his *Commedie* (1547). Lesser figures include Botero, Caro, Vittoria Colonna, Doni (whose *Marmi* are transmogriphied into *Marini* by a careless copyist or a careless printer), Guazzo, Garzoni, Groto, Guicciardini, Leone Ebreo, Alessandro Piccolomini (with four titles in Italian and others in Latin), Paruta, Sansovino, Sannazaro, Tullia d'Aragona, and Vasari. These represent, of course, a mere sampling. In addition to the comedies of Ariosto, other plays include those of Aretino—not, however, in Wolfe's edition—the *Sophonisba* of Caretto, Giraldi Cinthio's *Tragedie* (1551), Dolce's *Comedie et Tragedie* (1551), Guarini's *Pastor fido*, the anony-

36

mous *Gl'Inganni* (1562), and Trissino's *Sophonisba*. When we consider the comparative worth of the English and Italian theaters in the period, we can only conclude that someone who knew what he was about made the selections for Bodley's library; for the best of the Italian drama found its way into the collection.

Several of the titles in the appendix for the Arts are of special interest. Camillo Agrippa's *Scienza d'Arme* (1604), Tomaso Buoni's *Tesoro de' Proverbi* (1604), Annibale Caro's translation of Virgil's *Eneide* (1603), and Orlando Pescetti's *Proverbi italiani* (1603) indicate an active effort to keep abreast of recent publications. Others, such as Giulio Camillo's *Idea del Teatro* (1550), Giasone Denores' *Discorso intorno alla poesia* (1587), and Torquato Tasso's more famous *Discorso del Poema heroico* (not dated), perhaps reflect a conscious attention to critical theory. And a few are of interest simply as old friends: "John *Florio* his Italian & English Dictionarie *Lond.* 1598"[6] and the "Descrittione del Regno di Scotia, &c. per Petruc. *Ubaldini, Ant.* 158[8],"[7] which was the second of Wolfe's Ubaldini's to land on Bodley's shelves. The *Vite delle Donne illustri* (1591) had already been entered in the main body of the catalogue.[8]

With James's *Catalogus* the cup of our good fortune truly runneth over. For in 1620 he republished[9] and updated it, reorganized under a single alphabet, which permits us to see what was happening to the Bodleian's collection of Italian books in the intervening years. The total number of entries in the new catalogue appears to be much larger than the earlier one, and is now approaching twenty thousand items. Here we see that an attempt has obviously been made to keep accessions current, for the Catalogue and its appendix contain the titles of many books published in 1619 and a few in

---

[6]*Ibid.*, p. 603.

[7]*Ibid.*, p. 637.

[8]*Ibid.*, p. 403.

[9]*Catalogus Universalis Librorum in Bibliotheca Bodleiana* . . . Oxoniae, Excudebant Iohannes Lichfield, & Iacobus Short, Academiae Impensis Bodleianis. Anno 1620.

1620.[10] The new additions to titles of Italian authors already represented include Aretino's *Quattro Comedie* (1588—*now* in Wolfe's edition); Ariosto's *Cinque canti;* Bembo's *Asolani* (Venice, 1575); Boccaccio's *Nimphale d'Ameto* (1545); Dolce's *Osservationi nella volgar lingua* (1550); Florio's *Queen Anna's New World of Words,* Garzoni's *L'Huomo astratto* (1604) and *Piazza Universale;* Guazzo's *Civil conversatione* (1607); Alessandro Piccolomini's *La Raffaella* (1560); Machiavelli's *Discorsi* (1530), *Vita di Castruccio Castracani* (1532), and *L'Asino d'oro* (1588—Wolfe's edition); Parabosco's *Lettere amorose* (1584); Fabio Moretti's translation of Petrarch's disappointing *Africa* (1570); and Bernardo Segni's discourse *Sopra la Rhetorica et Poética d'Aristotile.* The list of such additions is long, and I abridge it merely to spare you the tedium of recited names.[11] But don't congratulate yourselves too heartily yet: there are more lists to come.

Among the very large number of authors and titles now included for the first time by James we find Isabella Andreini, *Lettere* (1612); Giovanni Astolfi, *Officina Historica* (1602); Strozzi Cigogna, *Palagio de gl'Incanti* (1605); the *Vocabulario de gli Academici della Crusca*; De Dominis, *Predica* (1617); Donato Giannotti, *De la Republica de Vinitiani* (not dated); three comedies—*La Gelosia, La Pinzochera, I Parentadi*—by A. F. Grazzini, called Il Lasca; several of Paolo Sarpi's tracts written during the Venetian's quarrel with Pope Paul V;[12] Flaminio Scala, *Il Teatro delle Favole rappre-*

---

[10]Among them: Alessandro Gatti's *La Caccia,* Patrick Hannay's *A Happy Husband,* William Basse's *Help to Discourse,* Owens' *Epigrams* (Englished), King James's *Works* (Latin), Samuel Purchas, *Microcosmus, or the history of man,* and Shelton's translation of Cervantes' *Don Quixote,* Part II (1620). Although the interval between catalogues shows the addition of half a dozen or more titles by Father Paul (= Paolo Sarpi), the Bodleian had apparently not yet acquired a printed copy of *The History of the Council of Trent* in any form.

[11]It should be added that the Appendix lists an edition of Bacon's *Saggi* (1619), "Gall. & Ital." —together with the *Sapienza de gli Antichi.*

[12]Not only Sarpi's, but many others', representing both sides of the

38

Portrait of Strozzi Cigogna from his *Palagio de gl'Incanti* (1605) Reproduced by permission from a copy in The Folger Shakespeare Library.

sentative (1611); and Sperone Speroni's *Dialoghi* (1596) and *Canace, tragedia* (1546). But Tasso, observe, is as yet represented only by his discourse *Del Poema eroico*; and, whereas Italian drama continues to be acquired, the Bodleian in 1620 has not a single play by Marlowe, Lyly, Shakespeare, Chapman, Webster, Jonson, or Beaumont and Fletcher.[13] 'Tis a mad world, my masters.

Casual mention was made, earlier, of the books of the poet, William Drummond of Hawthornden. These now repose—and have done so since 1627—in the Library of the University of Edinburgh. In turning from Bodley to Drummond, we are turning from what might be called an official or public collection to one which definitely reflects personal or private taste. Between the two there are, naturally, both correspondences and differences. We should expect a poet's tastes to exhibit pronounced leanings toward literature, and Drummond does not disappoint us.

Drummond also made doubly sure that there would be no future confusion as to the donor of his books: he published a catalogue[14] of his gifts, and he normally made upon the title page of each volume (often with a date) a separate notation, of which that in his Aretino may stand as a model: "Given to the College of King James in Edinb. by William Drummond." If there is, possibly, a lack of graciousness about these assertions of ownership, there is also (we may be grateful) no nonsense about the record. Drummond, an M.A. (1605) of Edinburgh, lived until 1649 and continued to present books to the university library long after the initial gift

quarrel. The inclusion of these titles no doubt reflects the general European interest in this famous contest; but it may also reflect the particular interest of the Librarian himself.

[13]Bodley's specific instructions to James to exclude plays and other "riffe-raffe bookes" in English—foreign ones were to be admitted for linguistic reasons—are amusingly dilated upon by Frederick S. Boas in his *Queen Elizabeth in Drama and Related Studies* (London, 1950), pp. 130ff.

[14]*Auctarium Bibliothecae Edinburgenae, sive Catalogus Librorum quos Gulielmus Drummondus ab Hawthornden Bibliothecae D.D.Q. Anno 1627*. Edinburgi, Excudebant Haeredes Andreae Hart, 1627.

of 1627. What must surely have been among the latest of these was an Italian version of Du Bartas, *La Divina Settimana* (1601), translated into *versi sciolti* by Ferrante Guisone. To keep it properly tethered, Drummond placed his signature at the top of the title page, wrote on the verso of the title page his characteristic inscription, "Given to the Colledge of Edenbrough by William Drummond of Hawthornden 1636," and repeated the record of gift, in Latin,[15] at the end of the text.

The Italian books entered in the *Auctarium* of 1627—and, except for seven or eight now catalogued as "missing," still preserved in the Library—number thirty-five; Drummond's identified later gifts of Italian books number twenty-two. Buying at such a rate, he would never have cornered the market. But in the matter of selection, a Bodley—or a Rosenbach—might well have been proud to be his associate.

His printed catalogue, by way of illustration, included Aretino, *Quattro Comedie* (1588—Wolfe's edition); Ariosto, *Orlando Furioso;*[16] Bembo, *Prose* (1540); Dolce, *Le Troiane Tragedia* (1583); the *Cecaria Tragicomedia* (1532) of "Epicuro Napolitano";[17] Gesualdo, *Plutosophia* (1592); Groto, *La Dalida Tragedia* (1595) and *Thesoro Comedia* (1599);[18] Guarini, *Pastor fido* (1603); Paolo Giovio, *Commentario de le Cose de Turchi* (1538); Machiavelli, *Discorsi;* "Il Petrar-

---

[15]Leaf 126 verso; no overscoring or marginal comments. The Library also possesses another Du Bartas in Italian: *La Divina Settimana: Cioè I Sette Giorni della Creation del Mondo. Tradotta di Rime Francese in verso sciolto Italiano* (Venetia, Gio. Battista Ciotti, 1593). This is bound in a Drummond brown calf binding standard to the collection but lacks markings or signatures. Did Drummond thus have *two* copies of Du Bartas in Italian and none in French or English? Queer.

[16]"Missing"—as are also Castiglione ("Baltasar Castellon. Il Cortesano" perhaps in Spanish), "Gratiano Partesana," David de Pomi Hebreo, M. Francesco Ricci, Tasso's *Gerusalemme liberata,* Antonio Zanobi, and Benedetto Zino.

[17]Also in Bodley's 1620 *Catalogus Universalis.* Drummond's copy carries a notation of purchase in Paris, 1608.

[18]Of all Drummond's Italian books I have examined, *La Dalida* shows most signs of close study. The copy has much of his distinctive *over*lining throughout and an occasional marginal note.

cha" (Venetia, 1596); Sannazaro, *Arcadia* (1589); M. A. de Dominis, *Scogli del Christiano Naufragio* (1618); and Tasso, *Il Rinaldo* and *Gerusalemme liberata*.[19]

This distinguished original grouping, with the other titles that make up the full number, was later signally supplemented by individual gifts of such works as Guazzo's *Civil conversatione* (1580), one of the most popular of all Italian books of the sixteenth century; an *Herodoto* (1539), in the translation of Matteo Maria Boiardo; several volumes of *Prediche* and other devotional writings of Bernardino Ochino; Boccaccio's *L'Amorosa Fiammetta* (1601); Dolce's *Amorosi ragionamenti* (1546); Florio's *Worlde of Wordes* (1598); Machiavelli's *Historie;* the noted *De' Secreti* of "Alexis of Piedmont" (i.e., Girolamo Ruscelli); and the Wolfe-printed Ubaldini, *Vita di Carlo Magno*. If Edinburgh was the "Athens of the North," Drummond went far toward making nearby Hawthornden its intellectual Venice.

ii

So far we have been looking at the spines of volumes on library shelves. It is time now to turn our attention in another direction. In addition to the activities of a semiprivate agent like John Bill and the thoroughly private purchasing activities of individual travelers to Italy—a Sidney, a Milton, or a Bishop Burnet—who supplied Renaissance Englishmen with Italian books? The answer is not to be found in *one* name, for various English booksellers visited Italy and the annual Frankfort Book Fair and returned with what were considered the most vendible imports.[20] But the surviving records of one

---

[19]See note 16, above.

[20]Naturally, the Frankfort and Leipzig bookfairs principally displayed German-printed books. Other countries did, however, have some representation. A table of interesting comparative figures for the Frankfort fair, covering a hundred-year period, is provided by James Westfall Thompson, *The Frankfort Book Fair* (Chicago: the Caxton Club, 1911), p. 116:

man's activities can throw a great deal of light upon the matter.

The man to whom I refer is Robert Martin, a London bookseller about whom very little is known beyond the fact that between 1633 and 1650 he issued several catalogues of books which he had imported from Italy.[21] I shall here be dealing with four of these catalogues, those for 1633, 1635, 1639, and 1640. Since these represent the whole or a large part of a bookseller's stock in trade, the successive issues reflect a certain carryover of titles.

Martin's first catalogue is entitled *Catalogus Librorum quos (in Ornamentum Reipublicae Literariae) non sine magnis Sumptibus & Labore, ex Italia selegit Robertus Martine, Bibliopola Londinensis: apud quem in Coemitero Divi Pauli prostant venales* (Londini, Aug. Mathewes, 1633).[22] Now, books *ex Italia selecti* are not necessarily books in Italian. In

Year	French	Dutch	Flemish	English	Italian
1564-69	152	2	247	---	381
1570-79	438	4	411	21	614
1580-89	464	48	349	27	492
1590-99	394	226	363	10	536
1600-09	564	384	619	36	1082
1610-19	918	798	781	151	559
1620-29	562	416	740	77	286
1630-39	252	665	486	15	34
1640-49	75	826	522	7	75
1650-59	128	865	474	27	40
1660-69	81	727	123	3	16

From 1564 to 1609, it will be observed, Italian-printed books, not necessarily in Italian (mostly, in fact, in Latin), dominated the importations; from the last decade shown to the closing of the Fair, Italian representation was so slight as to be negligible.

[21]See Dennis E. Rhodes, "Some Notes on the Import of Books from Italy," *Studi Secenteschi,* VII (1966), 131-138. Mr. Rhodes's article has been of use to me, though we approach the subject from rather different perspectives. Mr. Rhodes also discusses the importing activities of Henry Fetherstone and George Thomason, which I am not on this occasion prepared to pursue; the Fetherstone Catalogue (1628), in any event, contains no titles of books *in Italian.* I have, of course, examined the Martin catalogues independently.

[22]*STC* 17512.

fact, not a single book among those listed in Henry Fether-stone's *Catalogus librorum in diversi locis Italiae emptorum* (London, 1628) *is* in Italian. Martin's catalogues, however, while advertising books in various languages and from various countries, do contain many titles in Italian, which are here our sole concern. Following the cataloguing practice of his time, Martin divides his wares into categories: theology; a catch-all grouping which includes politics, history, geography, philosophy, "&c."; medicine; mathematics; law; music; "Libri varij Italici"; "Libri Hispanici" (with nine titles only); Greek; and Hebrew and other Orientalia. There are occasional Italian titles among the various categories and groupings: the forty entries devoted to "Libri de Architectura, & ad Bellum Spectantes," for instance, are, significantly, *all* in Italian—as are also virtually all those (over a hundred) in the Music category. The main entry of Italian books[23] contains some 330 titles, of which the following selection must stand as representative. Unfortunately for our curiosity, Martin indicates neither the printer nor the price.[24]

> Boccaccio della Genealogia de Gli Dei (1606)
> Bocalini de Raguali di Pernaso (1629)
> Botero della Ragion di stato (1619)
> Civill Conversatione di Guazzo (1621)
> Dante con L'espositione di Christoforo Landino (1529)
> — Idem con l'espositione di Bernardo Daniello (1568)
> Dieci libri di Pensieri diversi di Tassoni (1627)
> Grisoni ordini di Cavalcare (1620)
> Giraldi Cento novelle (1608)
> Il Pastor Fido (1621)
> Il Decamerone di Boccacio (1590, 1626)
> [Cartari] Imagini delli Dei (1626)
> Il Cortegiano de Castiglione (1573)
> Il Coralbo del Cavalier Biondi (1632)
> L'Eromena del Cavalier Biondi (1629)
> [Garzoni] La Piazza universale . . . (1616)
> L'arte vitraria del Antonio Ner[i] (1612)
> La Gierusalem Conquistata de Tasso (1628)

[23] Sigs. G2-H2.
[24] I follow Martin's spelling and capitalizations.

La Specchio [sic!] Rapita del Sig. Tassoni (1630)
Mascardi Prose volgari (1630)
Orlando furioso d'Ariosto (1619)
Proverbij Italiani de Orlandi Piscetti (1622)
Secreto D'Alessio (1628)

Probably I have omitted the very titles that some of you would have found of greatest interest; the process of selection plays hob with adequacy of coverage. The only remedy I can suggest is that you see the *Catalogus* for yourselves. But, lest you do not follow this counsel of perfection, before moving on to the other Martin catalogues, I must point out that this one contains both a large selection of *Lettere*—those of Aldo Manuzio, Tolomei, Bernardo Tasso, Franco, Guevara (*Italicè*), Caro, Guarini, Peranda, and Visdomini[25]—and half a dozen titles of recent date by the ruling Italian literary favorite, "Il Cavalier Marino": *La Lira* (1629), *Rime nuove* (1627), *Epitalami* (1628), *La Galeria* (1630), *Dicerie sacre* (1628), and *La Sampogna. Secentesimo,* we see, was making some headway in England.

Martin's second catalogue[26] is arranged in a fashion similar to that of his first, except that, following the section of "Libri Italici" (sigs. F3-G4) there is a short list of "Comedie & Tragedie Italici" (sigs. G4-G4verso). A considerable repetition of titles from the first catalogue suggests the possibility of sluggish sales during the two-year interval, though the number of changes and additions might lead to quite a different conclusion. An obvious attempt has been made to secure copies of the latest productions: many volumes are dated 1635, date of the catalogue itself. Among other changes and additions, Tassoni's *Secchia* now appears with the correct title and his *Considerationi sopra le Rime del Petrarcha*

---

[25]All on sig. G4.
[26]*Catalogus Librorum tam Impressorum quam Manuscriptorum quos ex Roma, Venetiis, aliisque Italiae locis, selegit Robertus Martine Bibliopola Londinensis. Apud quem vaeneunt in Coemiterio Divi Pauli.* Londini, Typis Iohannis Haviland, 1635. In addition to the printed books, this catalogue also has a list (sigs. K2-K3) of "Libri Manuscripti Italici."

(1609) has been added. Dante, however, though being offered in a new edition (of 1624) has suffered a strange seachange, being now advertised as "La Divina Comedie de Tante."[27] Bracciolini's *Scherno de gli Dei* (1626) appears for the first time, as do Sannazaro's *Arcadia* (1625), Diodati Solero's *La Nobile Conversatione* (1633), Francesco Pona's *La Galleria delle Donne Celebri* (1633), and G. B. Manso's *Dialoghi XII dell' Amore & della Bellezza* (1628). Giovanni Francesco Biondi's *Coralbo* and *Eromena* have now been joined by his collected *Opere* (1634) and *Donzella Desterrada* (1633); Marino's list has picked up the *Strage de gli Innocenti* (1633), the *Murtoleide* (1626), the *Lettere* (1629), and the resoundingly famous *Adone* (1626). A great favorite with the seventeenth-century English, the Marchese Virgilio Malvezzi, is represented by his *Davide Perseguitato* (1634), *Il Tarquinio Superbo* (1633), *Il Romulo* (1633), and *Il Ritratto del Privato Politico* (1635), every one of which, with others of his works, achieved translation into English before midcentury.

Of the forty-five plays advertised in their separate section, the following titles offer a fair sampling: Tasso, *Aminta* (1625); Bernardino Pino, *Gl'Ingiusti Sdegni* (1626); Francesco Bracciolini, *L'Amoroso Sdegno* (1626); G.-B. della Porta, *L'Astrologo* (1606) and *La Turca* (1606); Girolamo Parabosco, *Il Maranaco* (1586); Ercole Bentivoglio, *Il Geloso* (1627); Luigi Pasqualigo, *Il Fidele* (1589); Lodovico Dolce, *Ifigenea* (1597); Lelio Manzini, *Il Pellegrino Amante* (1623); Luigi Groto, *La Dalida* (1626); Maffeo Veniero, *Hidalba* (1623); and Sforza d'Oddi's *Il Duello d'Amore* (1622) and *Prigione d'Amore* (1630). Whatever Martin's other virtues, in the drama he was either less perceptive or less fortunate than the buyer for the nontheatrical Sir Thomas Bodley.

The third and most important Martin catalogue, that of 1639,[28] generally follows the pattern already established in

---

[27]Sig. G2 verso.
[28]*Catalogus librorum ex praecipuis Italiae Emporiis selectorum per*

the earlier ones, except that, after the regular (Latin) listing of medical books there follows an additional section of "Libri Medici Italici" (sigs. F2 verso-F3). What sale these may have had among the snobbish and learned medical men is not clear. Less exalted mortals must have found the increased accessibility of the *arcana medicorum* welcome, for Martin continued to use the new classification. Along with the carry-overs, there are in the new catalogue some interesting additions to the main section of "Libri Italici"; but the spectacular change occurs in the section devoted to "Comedie & Tragedie Italici" (sigs. H1 verso-H4). Here, the forty-five titles of 1635 have grown to a whopping 193—not, however, with any noticeable improvement of quality. Of the other changes and additions, Biondi's cribbed *Istoria delle Guerre Civili d'Inghilterra* (1637) now first appears, as does Guido Casoni's popular *Della Magia d'Amore* (1592; and Garzoni's *Piazza universale* is offered in the latest edition (1638). New, too, are Paolo Sarpi's *Historia dell' Inquisitione* (not dated), Mascardi's *Discorsi morali* (1638) and *Dell' Arte historica* (1636), Manso's *Vita di Torquato Tasso* (1621), and Malvezzi's *Discorsi sopra Cornelio Tacito* (1635). Both the dramatic and the nondramatic titles, we observe, reflect an increased attention to, and probably availability of, contemporary publications in Italian literature. Ironically, it is one of the distinguishing differences between the Tudor period and the Stuart period that when Italian literature was in a sagging state, the later age should show a more immediate response to it than did the former. Like many a modern university gone to pot, seventeenth-century Italy was living on a reputation of past greatness.

The fourth Martin catalogue [29] has a slightly different ar-

---

Robertum Martinum. *Apud quem venales habentur.* Londini, in Old Bayly, non procul ab Aquaeductu sub Venetiis. Typis Thomae Harper, 1639.

[29]*Catalogus librorum plurimis linguis scriptorum: de omni ferè facultate tractantium; ac è diversis Europae Regionibus congestorum: Prostant venales apud Robertum Martinum.* Londini, in Old Bayly, sub Venetiis. Typis Thomae Harper, 1640.

rangement but the content of Italian works differs very little from the third.

iii

From the catalogues and bookstalls of Robert Martin we now proceed to the examination of several composite collections of Italian books belonging to this and to a slightly earlier period. The first of these is recorded in the manuscript catalogue which Sir Edward Coke, Bacon's professional and matrimonial rival, had drawn up "shortly before his death on September 3, 1634."[30] The manuscript is headed "A Catalogue of All My Bookes both Printed and Manuscripts," has Coke's autograph in some twenty different places, and extends to 1227 entries, many of which embrace more than a single title. Entries 1–292 are classed as "Divinity"; 293–491, as "Books of the lawes"; 492–720, as "State matters, Chronicles, Histories, &c."; 721–783, "Philosophy, Rethoricke, Grammar, Lodgicke and Schoolebookes"; 784–817, "Phisicke and Naturall Philosophie"; 818–879, "books of poetrie"; 880–910, "Dictionaries"; 911–1227, a great miscellany of "severall sciences": political theory, heraldry and arms, pedigrees, cosmography, mathematics, trade, "Books of Warre and the like" (Nos. 1015–1032), tracts and discourses (1033–1199), and, finally, "Antiquities and Rarities." Italian books are scattered throughout and in several instances are grouped in their own labeled subdivisions: "Italian Books of Divinitie" (225–234), "Italian Books of Historie" (641–692), "Italian Books of Philologie and Grammar" (779–782), "Italian Books of Poetrye" and "Italian Playes" (869–879), "Italian Discourses and other Books &c" and "Italian Books of Letteres" (1098–1197). The entries are not always made in such a way as to guarantee absolute identification of the volume described, but my total count is 221 Italian books—approximately 18 per cent of the collection.

[30]W. O. Hassall, *A Catalogue of the Library of Sir Edward Coke* (New Haven, 1950). Yale Law Library Publications, no. 12, p. xi.

Such a high percentage of Italian books in any collection of this period is unusual and, as many of them are of humanistic or even belle-lettristic concern, would be absolutely astounding in the collection of the learned but not particularly humanistic Coke were there not a simple explanation. The collection is a composite aggregation, and it is unlikely that many of the Italian volumes—particularly the more literary items—represent the great lawyer's tastes. Coke's second wife was the widow of the heir to the estate of Sir Christopher Hatton,[31] Elizabeth's Lord Chancellor and favorite, and that marriage brought the Chancellor's books into Coke's possession. Many of the Italian volumes listed in Coke's "Catalogue" and still preserved at Holkham bear the armorial or initialed Hatton bindings or carry his signature on their title pages.[32]

Among the Italian books of divinity, together with several devotional works by Luis de Granada, is Hatton's well-perused copy of Beza's *Confessione della fede christiana* (1560); and among the "Approved Histories" are his copies of Guicciardini, *Historia d'Italia* (1574, 1580), Boccaccio's *Decamerone* (1582), Giovio's *Commentario delle cose de' Turchi* (1538) and *Istorie del suo tempo* (1581). Other histories, without indication of Hatton ownership, include Ubaldini's "The life of Charles the great" (= the Wolfe-printed *Vita di Carlo Magno,* 1581), G. M. Manelli's translation of Tacitus' *Vita di Giulio Agricola* (also Wolfe-printed, 1585), Pietro Giustiniano's *Historia Venetiana* (1571), and Sansovino's *Venetia città nobilissima et singolare* (1581, 1604). The only firmly Coke-associated entry among these fifty-two "Italian Books of Historie" is the curiously misplaced No. 656, Francesco Alunno's *Della Fabbrica del Mondo* (1584), really a dictionary, which carries his signature, "Edw: Coke" on the title page. In the section specifically reserved

---

[31]W. O. Hassall, *A Catalogue of the Library of Sir Edward Coke,* p. xiii.

[32]See, for example, Nos. 227, 229; 641, 642, 644, 646; 869, 871, 879; 1018, 1021; 1098, 1107, 1113, etc.

for Italian dictionaries, Coke had several: "Florioes Italian Dictionary" (No. 883 = *Q. Anna's New World of Words,* 1611), "William Thomas his Italian Grammar and Dictionary" (1550), Luc' Antonio Bevilacqua's *Vocabulario volgare et latino* (1583), and Alunno's *Ricchezze della lingua volgare* (1555 ?). In their grubby practicality these are probably authentic Coke.

Other notable entries, regardless of individual ownership, include No. 860, "Poet Dantes Workes" (1568 or 1578), *Il Petrarca con l'Espositione di M. Alessandro Velutello* (1584), Anguillara's *Metamorfosi di Ovidio* (1579), Tasso's *Gerusalemme Liberata* (1581), Ariosto's *Orlando* (1584), "Machiavells Mandragola" (No. 877: no further identification), Grazzini's *La Sibilla Comedia* (1582), Piccolomini's *Della sfera del mondo* (1576), Aurelio Cicuta's *Disciplina militare* (1572), the *Architettura* of Palladio (various copies: 1570, 1581, 1616) and of L. B. Alberti (1565), and Porcacchi's *L'isole piu famose del mondo* (1576). A few important items from the "Tracts and Discourses" section include Muzio's *Il Gentilhuomo* (1575), Tasso's *Il Forno overo della nobiltà* (No. 1102), "Machiavells golden Asse in 8°" (No. 1104: perhaps Wolfe's *L'asino d'oro,* 1588), Giannotti's *De la republica de Vinitiani* (1542), Equicola's *Libro di natura d'amore* (1563), Machiavelli's *Principe* (1537, 1541, 1584) and *Discorsi* (1537, 1584), Garzoni's *Teatro de' vari e diversi cervelli mondani* (1583), Aretino's *Ragionamenti* in Wolfe's printing of 1584 and 1588, Scipione Bargagli's *Imprese* (Siena, 1578), the *Opere Toscane di Luigi Alamanni* (1542), Bernardo Tasso's *L'Amadigi* (1581), and Trissino's *Italia liberata da Gotthi* (1547). The "Italian Books of Letters" (Nos. 1191–1197) include collections of Tasso, Porcacchi, Calmo, Bembo, Pino, Guevara, and Parabosco. Everything considered, a remarkable assemblage of Italian books.

The second of the composite collections is recorded in a list of 931 items set down in 1649 by Michael Roberts, successor to the dismissed Dr. Francis Mansell as Principal of

Jesus College, Oxford.[33] The list contains a record of books accumulated from the foundation of Jesus College (1571), supplemented notably by a gift of part of the library of Lord Herbert of Cherbury and by the unembittered Mansell's own library of nearly six hundred books. The books are listed (not very accurately) by size and by discipline, with medicine and theology looming large. Of the total, only thirty-seven can be firmly identified as Italian, and of these twenty-four were in the library of Lord Herbert. Most of the titles, as usual, are in Latin. Many of the Herbert items carry his initials and a notation of the purchase or binding price.[34]

The following are a few of the titles of chief interest to us:[35]

Vincenzo Galilei, *Dialogo . . . della musica antica et della moderna* (Florence, 1581) *H*

Andrea Palladio, *I quattro libri dell' architettura* (Venice, 1616) *H*

Giordano Bruno, *Del [infinito] universo et mondi* (Venice [i.e. London], 1584)[36]

Alessandro Piccolomini, (i) *Delle stelle fisse* (ii) *De la sfera del mondo* (Venice, 1552)

Filippo Gesualdo, *Plutosofia* (Padua, 1592) *H*

Thomas Morley, *Il primo libro delle ballette a cinque voci* (London, 1595)

G.-B. Marino, *Dicerie sacre* (Venice, 1628) *H*

Uberto Foglietta, *Della Republica di Genova* (Rome, 1559)

---

[33]C. J. Fordyce and T. M. Knox, "The Library of Jesus College, Oxford," *Oxford Bibliographical Society Proceedings & Papers*, V (1940: for 1936-39), 53-115.

[34]By way of illustration: For Giacomo Barozzi da Vignola's *Le due regole della prospettiva pratica* (Rome, 1611), folio, he paid £1.7s.; for Sperone Speroni's *Orationi . . . novamente poste in luce* (Venice, 1596), 4to, he paid 10s. Entries for such (comparatively) trifling amounts as the 4d. for Innocenzo Ringhieri's *Il Sole—dialogo* (Rome, 1550), are probably for binding.

[35]The books authenticated as belonging to Lord Herbert are indicated by an *H* after the publication date.

[36]"Missing" say Fordyce and Knox.

Desiderius Erasmus, *La moria, novamente in volgare tradotta*
[by Antonio Pellegrini] (Venice, 1544)
Girolamo Garimberto, *Della fortuna* (Venice, 1550) *H*
Alessandro Tassoni, *Dieci libri di pensieri diversi* (Venice,
1627) *H*

Before leaving Roberts' list of the Jesus College books, I
should like to call your attention to two further points. First,
the list also contains a copy of Robert Martin's *Catalogus librorum ex praecipuis Italiae emporiis selectorum* (1639);
and second, as a happy surprise, among Lord Herbert's
books are six titles by Partenio Etiro (whom you may recognize more readily, de-anagrammatized, as Pietro Aretino),
all purchased at five shillings apiece. The surprise is not that
the books are there, but that they represent an Aretino now
all but forgotten, an Aretino fallen into pious decline and
writing in the expectation of being rewarded with a cardinal's
cap. Included are *Dell' humanità del figliuolo di Dio* (1628),
Vita di Maria Vergine (1628), *Dello specchio delle opere di
Dio nello stato di Natura* (1629), *Vita di S. Caterina vergine
e martire* (1630), *Parafrasi sopra i sette salmi della penitenza
di David* (1629), and the *Vita di San Tomaso d'Aquino*
(1630). Not exactly what one might have expected from the
author of the *Ragionamenti* or the *Sonetti lussuriosi!*

The third and most important of the composite collections,
to which we now turn, has been called "the library of John,
Lord Lumley"—and he has, indeed, left a deep impress upon
it.[37] We cannot here go into the fascinating history of this collection,[38] which began as the library of Thomas Cranmer,

---

[37]Sears Jayne and Francis R. Johnson, eds., *The Lumley Library:
The Catalogue of 1609* (London, British Museum, 1956), p. 7: "The
library which Lumley thus inherited [in 1579, on the death of Arun-
del] was an extremely valuable collection of about 1000 printed
books and 150 manuscripts, but the library which he left at Nonesuch
at his own death [in 1609] was more than three times as large. In
spite of the important contributions of Cranmer and Arundel, the
collection here catalogued is therefore in a real sense the library of
John, Lord Lumley."
[38]*Ibid.*, pp. 1-26.

Archbishop of Canterbury; was confiscated in Mary's reign to Henry Fitzalan, twelfth Earl of Arundel and the Queen's Lord High Steward; passed from him to his son-in-law, John, Lord Lumley; thence, by uncertain means, upon Lumley's death, to Prince Henry; from him to the Old Royal Library; and, after many vicissitudes of losses, additions, sales, and piecemeal dispersion, came eventually by gift of George II into the British Museum. Fortunately for us, in 1596, at the very peak of its development, Lumley had it catalogued; and upon his death in 1609 that catalogue, with the subsequent additions, was recopied. Its modern editors describe it, with justification, as recording "the largest private library of the Elizabethan period."[39]

Most of the Lumley books, as we have come to expect, are in Latin. Only 187—"less than 7% of the entire library"— are in English. Next among the vernacular languages is Italian, with sixty-eight; then French, with fifty-eight; and only one or two in each of several other modern languages.[40] Choosing representative titles from a list in which virtually every entry deserves comment is particularly vexatious and unsatisfactory, but perhaps we may achieve some small measure of compensation by preserving in our list the eccentricities, inaccuracies, and polyglot uncertainties of Lumley's cataloguer:

957   *Alfonso Adriano della disciplina militare li: 3 Italice.* [Venice, 1556]

995   *Bandello de nouvelle in tre parte. Italice.* [Lucca, 1544]

1127   *Francisco Sansovino cento nouvelle scelte da i piu nobili scrittori. Italice bis.* [Venice, 1561]

1130   *Francisco Guicciardini de l'historia d'Italia li: 6. Ital: volumen primum, deest secundum.* [Florence, 1561]

---

[39]*Ibid.*, p. 1.

[40]*Ibid.*, p. 11. I use the statistics provided by Jayne and Johnson. My own count for the Italian runs slightly higher. In the subjoined list I follow the numbering, dating, and form of entry used by the editors of the *Catalogue.*

1141   *Giovanni Villani cittadini Fiorentini chroniche di Firenze. Italice.* [Venice, 1537]

1156   *Giovanni Boccaccii Decamerona ricorretto in Roma et emendato secundo l'ordine del sac concilio de Trento. Italice.* [Florence, 1573]

1181b   *Lodoico Guicciardini descrittione di tutti i poesi bassi. Italice.* [Antwerp, 1567]

1265   *Iosepho Hebreo della guerra Iudaica lib: 7 Italice.* [Venice, 1541]

1338   *Militia del gran duca di Thuschana capitoli ordini et privilegii della militia, dedicated to the Queene of England by Petruccio Ubaldino.* [Florence (i.e. London), 1597]

1347   *Nicolo Machiavelli discorse sopra la 1ᵐᵃ decadi Tito Livio libre 9. Italice.* [Florence, 1543]

1411   *Paolo Iovio gli elogi d'huomini illustri di guerra antichi et moderni, tradotto in volgare per Ludovico Domenichi.* [Venice, 1557]

1574   *Alessandro Piccolomini de la sfera del mondo lib: 4; de le stelle fisse lib: uno, Italice.* [Venice, 1552 or 1559]

1582   *Antonio Tibaldeo de Ferara* {*Soneti. Disperata. Egloghe.* {*Dialoghi. Epistolae. Capitoli.* { *Italice.* [Venice, 1500?]

1722   *Dante col sito et forma del l'inferno, Italice, carmine. Bis.* [Toscolano ? 1506 ?]

1768   *Francesco Alunno di Ferrara fabrica del mondo nella quale si contengono tutte le voci di Dante, del Petrarcha de Boccaccio et c., Italice.* [Venice, 1548]

1773   *Friderico Grisone gli ordini di cavalcare, Italice.* [Naples, 1550; Pesaro, 1556]

1929b   *Giovan. Batista Gelli Capricci, con dialogo del invidia, Italice.* [Florence, 1546]

2041   *Leone medico di natione Hebreo, et di poi fatto*

	christiano dialogi de amore, Italice. [Venice, 1541]
2042	*Leon Battista Albert della Pittura li: 3, tradotto di M: Ludovico Domenichi. Italice.* [Venice, 1547]
2043	*Lodovico Dolce Thyeste tragedia tratta de Seneca. Italice.* [Venice, 1543]
2047	*Leonardo Fioravanti Bolognese d'ello spechio di scientia universale, lib: tre. Italice.* [Venice, 1567 or 1572]
2090	*Nicolo Franco epistole volgare. Italice.* [Venice, 1542]
2104	*Opere del Bernia et mauro in terza rima. Italice.* [Venice, 1538]
2212	*Sebastiano Erizzo discorso sopra le Medaglie antique con la particular dichiaratione di molti reversi. Italice.* [Venice, 1559]

Noteworthy in the Lumley list are several features that do not emerge from the foregoing selection. One of these is the curious entry, No. 1609, *"Agreste de Ficaruolo commento sopra la prima ficata del padre Siceo, Italice, libro de Capriccii."* This is, of course, Caro's *Commento*,[41] but we would like to know whether it represents the original publication—which would surely have been a rarity in England—or a detached copy of the separately paged second part of the Wolfe-Aretino *Ragionamenti* of 1584. The irregular transcribing methods of the cataloguer, however, have put the question beyond final answering. A second feature is the almost complete absence of Italian drama, the lone play being Dolce's Senecan *Thyeste*. Those who relish oddity will perhaps see a wry compensation for this deficiency in the presence of Italian versions of several romances of chivalry: *Amadis, Primaleon,* and *Palmerin d' Oliva.*[42] They serve to

---

[41] The editors of the *Catalogue* assign it to Aretino and accept without challenge the "Bengodi" of Wolfe's 1584 title page.

[42] Thus entered in the Catalogue:
972 *Amadis de Gaule tria volumine Italice.*

remind us that the Elizabethans had not quite lost the tastes of their grandfathers or yet achieved a firm distinction between *storia* and *historia*. Finally, besides the one printed Ubaldini (No. 1338, above), there are also in the collection at least three of his manuscripts.[43] Since the Earl of Arundel was one of Ubaldini's patrons this is not surprising; but the fortuitous circumstance of their being in this particular collection has probably been the cause of their preservation.

If space permitted, something might be said about the Italian books in other collections of the Elizabethan and early Stuart periods. For although no one has yet discovered Shakespeare's catalogue of his library, from one source or another information is available concerning the Italian books owned (or read) by such striking figures as Sir Thomas Smith, Henry Percy (the "Wizard" Earl of Northumberland), Gabriel Harvey (Spenser's friend, the Cambridge orator and pedantic Italianist), Ben Jonson, John Morris (alias Iohannes Mauritius, Jean Maurice, and Giovanni Maurizio), Sir Kenelm Digby, and the authentic John Milton. Increasingly, toward the end of the seventeenth century, catalogues of libraries were preserved and published.[44] Not all of them are worthy of this attention, and fewer still are of interest for our special investigation. But, to round out our rapid survey, we need to turn now to several specimens belonging to this later period.

1405 *Primaleonis valorosi gesti, historia fabulosa. Italice.*

1409 *Palmerino d' Oliva historia fabulosa, vel Romanze. Italice.*

[43](No. 1465) *Scotiae descriptio a Deidonensi quodam anonymo, et Petrucci manu exscripta, et dedicata comite Arundel.* manuscript (= BM Ms Royal 13Aviii. The "anonymous native of Dundee" was Hector Boece); (No. 708) *Psalterium manuscriptum pulcherrime noviter.* of Petruccius dooinge (= BM Ms Royal 2Bix); and (No. 2146) *Petruccio Ubaldini his examples of wrytinge verie faire, dedicated to my lorde of Arundell.* manuscript (= BM Ms Royal 14A1).

[44]See, for instance, the catalogues represented by Wing *STC* B1985, B5726 (Lord Burghley's library), C1429, J113, L608, S4151, V765, W3612.

iv

The earliest among these, exactly at mid-century, is the catalogue of Sion College, London, prepared by its Librarian, the learned John Spencer.[45] This is arranged alphabetically on the pattern of the second Bodleian catalogue, which it patently follows at a very modest distance. Of the estimated 6500 titles most are in Latin, with the next largest number being in English. Italian and French titles, about equal in number, are few, not more than twenty apiece. The Spanish titles are even fewer. Choice items among the Italian books present are the *Orlando Furioso* (Venice, 1570), Diodati's translation of the Bible (1607), Boccalini's *Ragguagli* (1624), Castiglione's *Cortegiano* (Venice, 1549), Guicciardini's *Historia d'Italia* (1623), Petrarch in Latin and in an unspecified edition, and Tasso's *Il Goffredo* (Venice, 1595).

A much richer library, from the point of view of its Italian holdings—with a total of 328 titles in the exclusively Italian section of its auction catalogue[46]—was that of Arthur Annesley, Earl of Anglesey. No selection of titles could do justice to the richness of the collection or to the judicious balance between established and current reputations; we must be satisfied with a mere sampling of the names represented. These include Marino, Alunno, Dante, Ciro Spontone, Ubaldini, Paruta, Bembo, Francesco Guicciardini, Davila, Machiavelli, Giovio, Ammirato, Garzoni, Sarpi, many letterwriters, Giraldi Cinthio, Ripa, Botero, Polydore Vergil, Varchi, Biondi, Boccalini, Stefano Guazzo, Bernardo Tasso, Caro, Alessandro Piccolomini, Redi, Mascardi, Petrarca, Vittoria Colonna, Boccaccio, Fioravanti, Malvezzi, Torquato Tasso, etc. Among the books already discussed occur exemplars of Marino's *Adone;* Ubaldini's *Descrittione del Regno di Scotia* (Wolfe, 1588); the "Testina" (1550) edition of *Tutte le Opere di Nic. Machiavelli*; Garzoni's *Piazza univer-*

[45]*Catalogus Universalis Librorum Omnium in Bibliothecae Collegii Sionii apud Londinenses* . . . Londini, Rob. Leybourni, 1650.
[46]Pp. 89-96, *Bibliotheca Anglesiana* . . . 1686 (= Wing *STC* A3166).

sale, Theatro, and *Opere* (1605);[47] Guazzo's *Civil Conversazione* in a late Venetian edition of 1679; Sarpi's *Historia del Concilio Tridentino* (Geneva, 1629); Tasso's *Aminta* and Guarini's *Pastor fido*; and the Italian version of Bacon's *Essays, Saggi morali* (Milano, 1620).

Another auction catalogue belonging to the following year[48] is of interest, as are the earlier catalogues of Robert Martin, as representing the inventory of a bookseller's stock. Here, as with Martin, the books generally are in late or current editions. A special section of French books,[49] totaling 1407 items, is followed by a much smaller section of Italian books of 177 titles. This relationship perhaps shows the French to undue advantage but nevertheless reflects that decline of interest in Italian which Torriano was aware of in 1673.[50] The catalogue is ignorantly and carelessly put together, another indication of the rightness of Torriano's remarks; but if we close our eyes to glaring errors at every turn, we may gather some valuable information as to what were salable Italian titles in 1687. These include works of Davila, Boccaccio, Danielo Bartoli, Sarpi, Mascardi, Galileo, Tassoni (the *Pensieri diversi*), Biondi, Garzoni, Lorenzo Crasso, Tasso's *Aminta*, Leti, Aretino—perennially sought after—Ariosto, Boccalini, Marino, Sannazaro, and the *Opere scelte di Ferrante Pallavicino*, always sure to raise eyebrows and titillate fancies.

Far and away the most significant private library at the end of the seventeenth century was that of Dr. Francis Bernard, "Fellow of the College of Physicians, and Physician to S. Bartholomew's Hospital." His books, catalogued for auction

---

[47]This collective edition, published by the Venetian Meietti, included the *Theatro*, the *Sinagoga*, and the *Hospidale*. Daniel Tuvill, a rather unimaginative and free-handed borrower from his contemporaries, probably used it for the Garzonian touches in his two series of *Essays* (1608, 1609).

[48]*Catalogus Librorum Roberti Scott, Bibliopolae Regii Londiniensis* . . . 1687/8 (= Wing S2080).

[49]*Ibid.*, pp. 138-157.

[50]See above, p. 11.

"at the Doctor's late House in *Little Britain*," [51] were placed on sale on Tuesday, October 4, 1698, and offered such a selection as had never been seen before at a public auction in England. The sale must have continued for weeks. Almost exactly a century after the cataloguing of the rich Lumley assemblage, the Bernard catalogue repeats many titles found in the earlier listing and adds a truly representative selection of works coming out of Italy in the intervening hundred years. *Pars III*—the aristocratic Latin affectation lingered on for another hundred years—of the *Catalogue,* eighty-eight separately numbered pages, consists of two sections, viz. "Libri Italici Hispanici & Gallici" and "English Books in Divinity, History, &c." Both sections (like the rest of the *Catalogue*) divide the books into numbered lists according to size. The foreign-language section contains 71 folios, 351 quartos, and 741 octavos. Italian titles in the foreign-language section number 732—more than for any other language; and these, together with the other Italian titles scattered throughout the Catalogue, bring the Italian entries to approximately 900 titles. Nothing short of full reproduction can do justice to this incomparable collection; the following is a mere sampling, almost at random, of names represented: Trissino, Petrarca, B. Tasso, M. Guazzo, Marino, Vasari, Crasso, Bandello, Machiavelli, Biondi, Florio, Loredano, Garzoni, F. Guicciardini, Giovio, Dante, Ariosto, the "Passenger English & Italian" (London, 1612), Casoni, Erizzo, Tassoni, Baronio, Mascardi, Salviati, Guarini, Botero, Sansovino, Groto, Boccaccio, Sarpi, Redi, Lando (*Paradossi*), T. Tasso, Varchi, Dolce, Boiardo, Brusoni, F. Piccolomini, Aretino, Castiglione, Boccalini, Giraffi, Cartari, Torriano, Doni, Leti, F. Pallavicino, Diodati, Pescetti, Giraldi Cinthio, Ochino, Bruno, and so on, fascinatingly and endlessly.

Among the catalogues representing the libraries of more "literary" personages at the end of the century, a few are

---

[51] *A Catalogue of the Library of the late Learned Dr. Francis Bernard, Fellow of the College of Physicians, and Physician to S. Bartholomew's Hospital* . . . [London], 1698 (= Wing B1992).

worthy of at least brief notice.[52] The Italian books contained in the extensive Pepysian collection, preserved virtually intact in Magdalene College, Cambridge, are surprisingly few. For our purposes the libraries of two of Pepys's distinguished younger contemporaries will serve much better—those of John Locke and William Congreve.

v

Locke's library, assembled over many years in various places, was subjected to many shiftings and some losses; it reached its fullest form and was finally gathered into one place only during the last years of his life. According to the count provided by the modern editors of his final catalogue,[53] Locke's library eventually contained 3,641 titles. By far the greatest percentage of these titles, 23.8 percent, pertained to theology (a hard fact for the the modern mind to digest); 10.1 percent to Classical literature (Latin and Greek); and only 5.8 percent (in all vernaculars) to modern literature. Of the major linguistic groupings, 39.2 percent of the titles were in English, 36.5 percent in Latin (even this was a situation which would have been drastically reversed fifty years earlier), 18.3 percent in French, and a sharply trailing 2.6 percent in Italian. Curiously, Italian-printed books in Locke's library had almost the same dismal percentage, 2.9 percent, with Britain (45 percent), the Netherlands (19.6 percent), and France (16.9 percent) far in the lead.[54]

Yet, notwithstanding the overweight of French among the modern foreign languages, Locke's selection of Italian authors and works—95 titles—is extremely interesting.

Although reasonably supplied with Classical and English drama, Locke's library contains only a few titles in Italian drama: an unidentified *Annibale tragicomedia* (No. 97a),

[52]Jonathan Swift's library is given fleeting attention below, p. 86n.
[53]John Harrison and Peter Laslett, eds., *The Library of John Locke* (Oxford, 1965). Oxford Bibliographical Society Publications, new ser., vol. XIII.
[54]*Ibid.*, pp. 18-20.

an unidentified volume of *Comedie* (No. 816), Guarini's *Pastor fido* (Venice, 1602), Silvano Razzi's *Comedie* (Firenze, 1565), and Tasso's *Aminta* (Venetia, 1609) make up the lot. On the other hand, there are present a surprising number of works by some of the more scandalous or sensational modern writers. The moderately respectable Boccalini is there with four titles (Nos. 362–365): *La bilancia politica* (1678), the *Commentarii sopra Tacito* (1677), the *Pietra del paragone* (1652), and the amusing and caustic *Ragguagli di Parnaso* (1612). Gregorio Leti is represented by the *Vita di Donna Olimpia Maldachini* (No. 1349) and five other titles (Nos. 1719–22, 2089); Ferrante Pallavicino by his *Opere scelte* (Villafranca, 1666) and several separate titles (Nos. 2174–78a); and the chatty Vittorio Siri by both his gossipy *Mercurio* and *Memorie recondite* (Nos. 2686–87). On the more respectable levels of history Locke can boast of Cardinal Bentivoglio's *Lettere* and *Memorie* (Nos. 268, 268a); Davila's *Guerre civili di Francia* (No. 927); two copies of Guicciardini's *Historia d'Italia* (Nos. 1357–58); Juan Gonzalez de Mendoza's *Historia della China* in the original Roman edition (No. 1965); and Sarpi's *Opere, Lettere, Historia del Concilio Tridentino* (two editions), and *Historia dell' Inquisitione* (Nos. 2182–2185).[55]

In *belles lettres* the collection can show two copies of Aretino's *Ragionamenti* (Nos. 112, 112a), one being Wolfe's edition of 1584; Boccaccio's *Il filocopo* (No. 361); the *Rime et prose* (No. 613) of Monsignor della Casa; Castiglione's *Cortegiano* (No. 626); Guazzo's *Civil conversatione* in Latin and Italian (No. 1351); *Il Petrarcha* (Venice, 1564: No. 2273); and Tasso's *Gerusalemme liberata* (Casalmaggiore, 1581: No. 2834). Other works of varied interest include

---

[55]This pronounced interest in Sarpi is just about matched, *sans* the Italian texts, by the library of Locke's exact contemporary, the Reverend Thomas Plume, of Maldon in Essex; see *Catalogue of the Plume Library,* comp. S. G. Deed and Jane Francis (Maldon, 1959), p. 129. Although the Plume collection is about twice the size of Locke's, and although it contains many translations from the Italian, along with Latin works by Italian authors, I cannot find that it contains a single book *in Italian.*

Lorenzeo Magalotti's *Saggi di naturali sperienze* (No. 722), which he reported as Secretary for the Accademia del Cimento; the *Vocabolario degli Academici della Crusca* (No. 894); seven works by Leonardo Fioravanti, including two copies of the *Specchio di scientia universale* (Nos. 1123–1130); the Italian Hakluyt, G. B. Ramusio, *Delle navigationi et viaggi* (No. 2438), in three folio volumes; Francesco Redi's *Esperienze intorno a diverse cose naturali* (No. 2454a); a *Nuovo Testamento* (No. 2872) in the version of Diodati; and the *Viaggi* (No. 3046) of Pietro della Valle.

It is the library, we perceive, of no narrow specialist or Dr. Dryasdust.

Congreve's library[56] is much smaller than Locke's and much more distinctly the library of a fine gentleman and *littérateur*.[57] With his own catalogue, dating from the last year of his life, we also move slightly beyond our chronological limit. Nevertheless, it is worth examining as a reflection of educated literary taste at the close of the seventeenth century. English titles predominate, though "a full fourth of his library [is] in French, nearly a fifth in Latin, and a goodly number of volumes in Greek."[58] Items in Italian account for only fourteen out of 659, barely more than 2 percent. There is no Ariosto in any form, no Bembo, no Dante, no Machiavelli, no Guicciardini. Congreve's Boccaccio (the *Decamerone*) is in English and in French, his one Gregorio Leti in French, his Sannazaro in Latin, and his Sarpi is Brent's translation of *The History of the Council of Trent,* published, as mentioned earlier, by John Bill in 1620. Although his library, as we might expect, is rich in the drama, his only Italian dramatic pieces are Tasso's *Aminta* (No. 29), Bonarelli's *Filli di Sciro* (No. 253), Guarini's *Pastor fido* (No. 484), and Flaminio Scala's *scenarii, the Teatro delle Favole rappresentative* (No. 600). He has two editions of Marino's *Adone* (Paris, 1623; Amsterdam, 1678), the *Novelas ejemplares* of Cervantes in

---

[56]See John C. Hodges, *The Library of William Congreve* (New York, 1955).

[57]*Ibid.*, p. 15—in Jacob Tonson's phrase, "genteel & well chosen."

[58]*Ibid.*, p. 13.

an Italian translation (Venice, 1626), Tasso's *Gierusalemme Liberata* (Amsterdam, 1678), and, at a surprisingly late date, Wolfe's 1584 printing of Aretino's *Ragionamenti*.

But it is only this last belated echo of the past that reminds us of the ground we have covered. We have moved into a different world.

III

Horner's Plum: Tomaso Garzoni

When it first became clear that the date for this lecture was to fall on All Fools' day, it seemed only appropriate that the speaker make some effort to recognize the gravity of the situation. The choice of the present topic was the result—I might almost say, the inevitable result. For Garzoni, in the early years of the century and a half in which we have concentrated our interest, celebrated fools most festively and left behind him, at his early death—he was barely forty—a legacy of wisdom and laughter. Or perhaps you think those two terms synonymous.

If you have been listening with befitting attention to the preceding lectures, Garzoni's name and some of the titles of his works will already have become familiar to you. In the period with which we have been dealing, they would have been instantly meaningful to anyone in the least acquainted with Italian letters. Nowadays, perhaps even a few Italians might be momentarily puzzled if asked to identify him; but he is still worth knowing.

Ottaviano Garzoni[1] was born, as his title pages constantly proclaim, in Bagnacavallo, and at just the middle of the *Cinquecento*, in 1549. After studying law in Ferrara and Siena, he entered holy orders in 1566, assuming the name of Tomaso. He lived thereafter a quiet life of eager and wide-ranging study, observing of his fellowmen, editing and translating religious texts, and composing his encyclopedic commentaries

---

[1] The prime (but exceedingly brief) account of his life is that given by his brother, Bartolomeo, in the "Laconismo vitale" prefixed to *Il Serraglio de gli Stupori del Mondo, di Tomaso Garzoni da Bagnacavallo* (Venetia, 1613), sig. a4 verso.

65

on human foibles and vanities. He was a bookish man, a consumer and producer of books,[2] in short, a natural target for bibliographers.

Suppressing the piety that would normally lead us to dwell on those works of his better nature—his theological commentaries, his translating of Denis the Carthusian and editing of Hugh of St. Victor,[3] or even his *Vite delle donne illustri della scrittura sacra* (1588)—we will look at that series of his secular works which met such resounding acclaim at home and abroad in his own day and for half a century after. And in the process, let us ask ourselves this bipronged question. What interest had Englishmen in those books, and how was that interest manifested?

i

A bare listing of titles will serve to bring the relevant works before us and later we shall give them separate attention. These are, in order of publication, *Il Theatro de' vari, e diversi cervelli mondani* (1583), *La Piazza universale di tutte le professioni del mondo* (1585), *L'Hospidale de' pazzi incurabili* (1586), and *La Sinagoga de gl'Ignoranti* (1589), all published within the lifetime of the author. Three others were published posthumously: *Il mirabile cornucopia consolatorio* (1601), *L'Huomo astratto* (1604), and *Il Serraglio de gli stupori del mondo* (1613).

Since it is neither quite cricket nor good manners to brush the ladies aside and allow fools to rush in where those angels have not been permitted to tread, let us pay at least our hasty respects to the *Lives of the Illustrious Women of Holy Writ.*

[2] Besides the ample witness of the books he wrote, his brother—possibly a prejudiced witness—declares concerning his reading: "Non fù Historico tra latini, e volgari da lui non veduto, non Oratore, non Poeta, ove in queste professioni fù tanto singolare, che al sicuro hebbe pochi pari." *Ibid.*, sig. bl.

[3] See *Hugonis de S. Victore . . . Opere omnia tribus tomis digesta, . . . Venetiis, J. B. Somaschum, 1588.* Other eds.: Mainz, 1617; Cologne, 1621. G. Draud, *Bibliotheca Classica* (1625), lists a Venetian edition of 1581

Something is lost in citing this work, as is usually done, by the short form of its title, for the volume contains an *Aggiunta delle vite delle donne oscure, & laide dell'uno, e l'altro Testamento,* and ends with a characteristic Renaissance *Discorso sopra la Nobiltà delle Donne.* The *Lives,* needless to say, are almost wholly fanciful, a kernel of biblical data[4] wrapped in a great gauzy fluff of cotton-candy moralizing, permitting the author to exhibit simultaneously his virtue and his virtuosity. There is no shadow of relieving wit or ironic detachment; all is the dreariest of sermonizing. On the proper side of the ledger are to be seen lives of Mother Eve, of Leah and Rachel, of Anna the mother of Samuel; of the Queen of Sheba, of the Shunamite woman, of Tobias' demon-haunted Sara; of Judith, Susanna, and the mother of the Maccabees; of Elizabeth, of Martha, of Mary Magdalene, and, to sum up the "good" lives, that of the Virgin Mary. On the other side of the account the reader may be edified by the finger-wagging sketches of the Egyptian woman who attempted to seduce Joseph, of Samson's first wife, the woman of Timna, of Dalila, of Jezebel, and of the wicked Herodias.

The book had, as far as I can discover, only one edition; and although Milton might conceivably have been attracted by the psychology of the sketches of Eve, Dalila, and the woman of Timna—especially by the feminine tears and the temptation *motif* in all three—I think he would probably still have been able to write *Paradise Lost* and *Samson Agonistes* without assistance from Garzoni.

Having paid our respects to the ladies, we may now return to our proper starting point, Garzoni's first book, the *Theatro*

---

[4] *Le Vite delle donne illustri della scrittura sacra* . . . (Venetia, G. B. Somasco, 1588). The author's own conception of his performance, not often achieved in this work or elsewhere, is expressed at the beginning of the "Vita della Regina Saba" (p. 57): ". . . dirò brevemente di lei qualche cosa seguendo la verità della scrittura sacra (come nelle vite antecedenti ho fatto) senza meschiare alcune cose leggieri, e di poca fede, che parte nell'historia scolastica, e parte in altri si ritrovano, essendo io stato sempre piu vago della sincerità dell'historia, benche breve, che della copia di diversi fatti poco sinceri, e fedeli."

de' vari, e diversi cervelli mondani. This was one of his more successful books.[5] Besides its eleven editions in Italian between 1583 and 1617, it was quickly translated into French (by Gabriel Chappuys) and into Spanish. Like those which were to follow, it shows markedly the author's inherited Aristotelian tendency to categorize and his tedious Schoolman's taste for subdivision and infinite distinction. Fortunately, he is less dully systematic than his cumbersomely erected frameworks might seem to require. Nevertheless, the structural, or architectural, image is kept in the forefront of our attention, both in title and in text: Garzoni is *constructing* a theater. The idea becomes almost obsessive in the titles and plans of later works—his *Piazze,* hospitals, synagogues, palaces.

The raw building materials from which he will erect his "theater" or which, we might say, will be admitted to fill a part of it, are human *cervelli,* or wits (or, even more literally, brains). These are of six general sorts, each capable of infinite variety: *Cervelli, Cervelloni, Cervelluzzi, Cervelletti, Cervellini,* and *Cervellazzi.*[6] They will be placed within the "theater" in better or worse positions as they are adjudged to be good or bad. Since, in Garzoni's view, most of them are not highly commendable—*"Stultorum infinitus est numerus"*[7]—there will be no lack of material. In fact, he requires fifty-five discourses, or chapters, to deal with all the varieties of Big-Brains, Little-Brains, Geniuses, Pea-Brains, Wicked-Brains, Brain-Trusters, Madmen, Screwballs, Clever-Boys, and Wits that the Devil Himself will have nothing to do with. And sometimes he grows a little weary of his own everlasting *distinguo,* as when he speaks of *Cervellazzi Vitiosi in genere:*

---

[5] *Il Theatro de vari, e diversi cervelli mondani . . .* (Venetia, Paolo Zanfretti, 1583). Other Italian editions: Venetia, 1585 (octavo and quarto); Ferrara, 1586; Venetia, 1588 (octavo and quarto), 1591, 1595, 1598, 1605, 1617. In French as *Le Théâtre des divers cerveaux du monde . . . traduict d'Italien, par G.C.D.T.* (Paris, Jean Houzé, 1586); in Spanish as *El theatro de ingenios y Sinagoga de ignorantes, de Thomas Garçon . . . Puesto en español por Iayme Rebullosa . . .* (Barcelona, Iayme Cendrat, 1600).

[6] *Theatro,* p. 15.

[7] Quoted in "Discorso LI," *ibid.,* p. 134.

I have judged it a necessary and convenient thing to treat in this place of harmful madcaps in general. For, just as we have earlier had occasion to speak of virtuous wits under a common and general designation so as not to have cause to treat endlessly of infinite particulars, so I hold and esteem it a fitting and necessary thing, in order not to be bogged down forever with the unending supply of madcap wags who are found in the world, to assign here in this our theater a common seat to all the varieties unnamed, which shall be called the Seat of the Vicious Wits.[8]

This presentation of all sorts and conditions of human minds and dispositions is akin to those sketches of types which were to become favorites with the English and French in the seventeenth century, the Theophrastan "characters." There is a kinship, too, with those lopsided caricatures of humanity which Ben Jonson chose to call "humors." Sometimes, as with the discourses on alchemists and astrologers,[9] it is a profession whose practitioners are pilloried in general terms—a method anticipating that of Garzoni's second book. In describing the "Cervellazzi Alchimistici," Garzoni allows himself to burst into a little exclamatory heat:

As they appear to you, then, charged with smoke, full of heat, smeared with pitch, stinking of sulphur, with their eyes watery, their brows besweated, noses dripping, with hands and faces stained, with dirtied clothes, with aching heads and shaking members, but above all with empty purse—here they have shown to you their great secret of converting, of transmuting, and of making the true metamorphosis, who from being *al*chemists become *bad*chemists, from being physicians (*medici*) become beggars (*mendici*), from being herbmen become colliers, to the laughter, jesting, and satisfaction of everyone. In sum, I have always heard it said that all alchemists are rich only in three things: in smoke, in

---

[8]*Ibid.*, "Discorso XLIII," p. 110. I am, alas, responsible for all translations from Garzoni except those from the *Hospidale*.

[9]*Ibid.*, Discourses XLIX and L, respectively. Garzoni treats these same professions again (and at greater length) in the *Piazza universale,* Discourses XIII and XXXIX.

hope, and poverty. O madness beyond all madness, O folly which knows no mean in spending, lacks control in purchasing, has no system in disposal, has no measure in working, has no knowledge of returning, no foundation in beginning, and no perfection in ending![10]

Ben Jonson may not have known this *Discorso,* but he could have learned something from it. The *copia* in which it flows is typical, even though its concentration is not. A discourse which scatters its shot over a wider target is No. LIII: *De' Cervellazzi, Terribili, indomiti, diavolosi, intraversati, precipitosi, trapanati, bizzari, bislacchi, balzani, & helterocliti*—whose common denominator is, like Milton's Satan, their "constant will to do evil, never to do good." Some of these citizens are my neighbors.

In the *Theatro,* as in all his works, Garzoni is an indefatigable citer of authorities, ancient and modern, so that he often supplies a selective bibliography for the topic under discussion. His quotations from the poets, though brief, are frequent and catholic in range. English readers of his books (and we have seen that they were not a few) would have had their attention constantly directed by such references to both the established classics and the currently popular writers in Italian, often to the tune of a quietly intruded evaluating adjective: "il divino Ariosto," "il gentil Molza," and "il gentil Remigio Fiorentino," "il dottissimo Alciato," "il profondo Toscano Poeta," or "il dottissimo Dante." Not all his critical estimates exude such sweetness and light: he includes among the "Cervellazzi maligni & maldicenti," those "new Momuses and Zoiluses," Pietro Aretino, Niccolò Franco, and Ortensio Lando, along with "molti altri." He scatters largesse of names everywhere, with snippets of verse beside them: Vittoria Colonna, Monsignor Giovanni Guidiccioni, Giuliano Goselini, Benedetto Varchi, Luigi Groto, "il Petrarca," Angelo di Costanzo, Giovanni Andrea dell'Anguillara, Laura Terracina, Pietro Bembo, Giacopo Bonfadio, Giovanni Boc-

[10]*Theatro,* p. 128.

70

caccio—great and small, cheek by jowl in endless succession. Garzoni is a one-man publicity campaigner for Italian literature.[11]

As Garzoni's eye surveys mankind from China to Peru, taking us along in his sweeping view, he is led to exclaim, "Dio immortale, quanti cervelli sono al mondo!"[12] And when he considers the pretentious fourflushers among them (outnumbering honest men a hundred to one), he quietly observes, "Veggio quasi tutto il Theatro pieno di questi irrationali."[13] He knows not whether to weep or to laugh over this mixed bag, and neither do we. The more we accompany him, however, the more we are again and again reminded of an old friend, *The Anatomy of Melancholy*. Robert Burton does not cite Garzoni among *his* authorities, and if he knew him at all it is not certain that he knew this book. But if that roving bookman's eye of his ever did fall upon it, in his own or in Bodley's library, he could only have been delighted with Discourse XLVIII, "Of Melancholy Great Minds." And an even greater than he, looking over his shoulder, might have picked up a crumb or two of information from the discourse, for the second half of it concerns that melancholic Athenian, Timon.

The "Still resolute John Florio," who *does* cite four of Garzoni's books among his sources, when he attempts to set down their titles might better be described as the "still mud-

---

[11]The text is already burdened with more names than it can bear, but a passage in "Discorso XXXIV" is so characteristic that it must be recorded. In speaking of the poets that his "Cervelloni Universali industriosi, & ingegnosi" will be readily conversant with—or at least *about*—after listing the Ancients, Garzoni adds:

> Fra volgari; i Sonetti del Petrarca, del Bembo, del Veniero, del Guidiccione, del Varchi, del Benaglio, del Capello, del Molza, del Binaschi, del Bŏfadio, del Dolce, del Domenichi, d'Annibal Caro, del Tasso, del Goselino: I Madrigali del Parabosco, e del Cieco d'Adria. Gli versi sdruccioli del Sannazaro. I Terzetti del Signor Fabio Galeota. i Poemi compiti dell'Ariosto, & dell'Anguillara, con tanti altri, che ne la penna, nè il dire ponno sufficientemente isprimere. [*Theatro*, p. 77]

[12]*Theatro*, p. 14.
[13]*Ibid.*, p. 66.

dled-headed" Florio, for in both his *Worlde of Wordes* (1598) and *Queen Anna's New World of Words* (1611)[14] he refers to Garzoni's *Hospidale degli Ignoranti* and *Sinagoga de' Pazzi*. Nor is he much more helpful in penetrating the *sfumature* of Garzoni's labels: of the six categorizing terms he defines only *cervello, cervellino,* and *cervellaccio* (Garzoni's *cervellazzo*).

Like many another authorial parent patting his brainchild on the head and sending it hesitantly forth with a "Goe, littel boke," Garzoni releases the *Theatro* with a promise of more to come if the reception of the first warrants it. "Well, here it is," he says in effect,

> brought to that perfection and conclusion which Divine Grace has permitted it. Wherefore, rejoicing, we offer it, perfect or imperfect as it may be, to the sight of all, hoping that if perchance the form do not please the most perceptive judgement of the spectators, at least by its subject matter and by the novelty of fancy in the Architect it shall prove meritorious and acceptable in the sight of such persons. Which, if it happens so, with God's favor the world shall presently rejoice in a rare, gay, and priceless view of a more considerable, more learned, and more delightful fabrication. Meanwhile, let it take profit in peace from this modest little Theater, awaiting the presentation of that imposing monument which is already erected in the mind of this same Author.[15]

ii

The promise made at the end of the *Theatro* Garzoni fulfilled two years later with the publication of *La Piazza universale di tutte le professioni del mondo* (1585). This, his

[14]See "The names of the Authors and Books that have been read of purpose for the collecting of this Dictionarie," prefixed to both volumes.

[15]*Theatro,* p. 144. For copies of the *Theatro* known to have been in England during the period under survey, see above, pp. 36, 50, 58. Other copies are recorded in the libraries represented by Wing *STC* A3166 (two copies), B1985, S2080.

most popular and probably his most useful book, was issued repeatedly in Italian down to 1675, was translated into German and Latin, and was partly translated, partly adapted for Spaniards by the celebrated Doctor Christoval Suarez de Figueroa, whose version was reprinted as late as 1733.[16]

The *Piazza* is indeed that more imposing monument which the writer had promised. The basic scheme is the same as in the *Theatro:* a structure whose mass is built up of individual blocks of observations on a series of loosely related topics, this time the widely varied ways in which the *cervelli* of the former work set themselves to the task of keeping the wolf from the door, getting the world's business done, or merely diverting themselves. The discourses are generally longer than those in the *Theatro,* and there are more of them—one hundred fifty-four. Some of the "professions" are not professions at all, and some repeat matter already treated in the

---

[16]*La Piazza universale di tutte le professioni del mondo . . .* (Venetia, Giovanni Battista Somascho, 1585). I follow Marino Parenti, *Prime edizioni italiane,* in citing this as the first edition. An alleged earlier edition (Venetia, Ziletti, 1584), if it exists, I have not seen. Other editions in Italian: Venetia, 1586, 1587, 1588, 1589 (all by Somascho), 1592 (Paolo Meietti), 1593 (Heredi di G. B. Somasco), 1595 (Vincenzo Somasco), 1596, 1599 (Roberto Meietti), 1601; Serravalle di Venetia, 1604, 1605 (R. Meietti); Venetia, 1610, 1611 (Marco Claseri), 1612, 1616 (Oliviero Alberti), 1617 (Giorgio Valenti & Antonio Giuliani), 1626 (Pietro Maria Bertano), 1638, 1639, 1651 ("il Barezzi"), 1665 (Michiel Miloco), 1675 (Antonio Boso). In Latin: *T. Garzoni . . . Emporii emporium, sive Piazza universale . . . Opera omnia universalem doctrinam politicam aliosque discursus historico-philologicos complectentia. In tres libros distributa. Interprete N. Bello* [i.e., M.C. Lundorp] *. . .* (Francofurti, 1623-24). In German: *Piazza universale, das ist: Allgemeiner Schauwplatz, oder Marckt, und Zusammenkunfft aller Professionen, Künsten, Geschäfften, Händen und Handtwercken so in der gantzen Welt* (Franckfurt am Mayn, N. Hoffman, 1619): other eds., Frankfort, 1620 (L. Jennis), 1626, 1641 (W. Hoffmann), 1646, 1659 (M. Merian). In Spanish: *Plaza universal de todas ciencias y artes . . .* (Madrid, L. Sanchez, 1615); Perpiñan (Luys Roure), 1629/30; Madrid, 1733. C. G. Jöcher, *Allgemeines Gelehrten-Lexicon* (repr. Hildesheim, 1961), s.v. "Garzoni," says that the Piazza was translated into French as *La place de toutes les professions du monde,* but he gives no further particulars, and I have not been able to trace such a translation elsewhere.

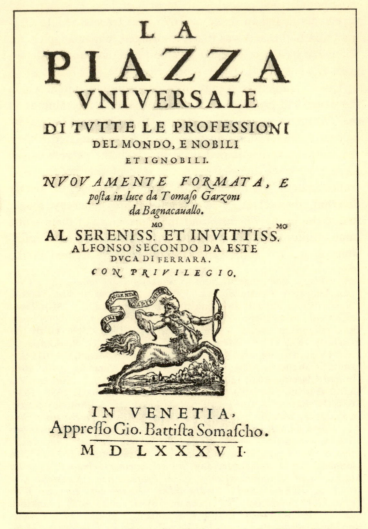

Title page of Tomaso Garzoni's principal work, *La Piazza Universale*. The Somaschi family were his chief printers. Printed by permission from a copy in The Folger Shakespeare Library.

Theatro. All of them allow for the greatest liberty of digression. Garzoni simply looks about and sees Man in Action. Then he talks about what he sees, or gleans from books.

A preliminary discourse,[17] entitled "Discorso universale in lode delle Scienze, & dell'Arti Liberali, & Mecaniche in commune," together with the author's prefatory address [18] to the "nobilissimi spettatori" gives the rationale for assembling in one place this passing show of *homo laborans*. More than half the discourses treat not of a single profession but of several related ones lumped together, as does, for instance, "Discorso CIII," which concerns those having to do with the woolen trade: woolworkers, wool manufacturers, woolens merchandisers, wool carders (or beaters), owners of wool-carding works, shearers, bolting-sievers, simple carders, fullers, woolen-cleaners, cloth trimmers, patchers, spinners, warpers, weavers, carders (again!), pieceworkers, wool dyers, nailers, clothworkers, bed-coverlet makers, coarse-serge makers, upholsterers, cap makers, hair workers, and mattress makers. Everybody is there but the sheep.

The immediately following Discourse, No. CIV,[19] will serve as well as any other to illustrate the utter lack of systematic arrangement or sequence, for it treats "De' Comici, e Tragedi, cosí Auttori, come Recitatori, cioè de gli Histrioni." Although recording the low esteem in which actors were generally held during antiquity, Garzoni here praises a number of contemporary actors and actresses, including Isabella Andreini and "that worthy Lydia from my own native place." Incidentally, he mentions among modern writers of tragedies and comedies who "hanno composto egregiamente," Ariosto, Ercole Bentivoglio, Alessandro Piccolomini, Bernardino Pino, Lodovico Dolce, Giangiorgio Trissino, and Giambattista Giraldi Cinthio. English readers in the reign of Charles I could have purchased plays by any of these writers at the shop of Robert Martin, bookseller in London, "at the Venice in the Old Bayly."

---

[17]*Piazza*, pp. 11b-14b.
[18]*Ibid.*, pp. 10b-11a.
[19]*Ibid.*, pp. 319b-321b.

Some of the "professions" about which Garzoni chooses to write would not be found in the yellow pages of a modern telephone directory. What, for instance, would be the profession represented by Discourse No. IX, "De Professori d'Imprese, et d'Emblemi," which might once have been meaningful, or Discourse No. XIX, "De'nobilisti, overo Gentilhuomini," or No. XXI, "De l'Arte di Raimondo Lullio"? Something might be made, a little distantly, of the second part of No. LXIII, "De gli Heretici, et de gli Inquisitori," but where, nowadays, will you find anyone "professing" *heresy*? And where—unless among Congressmen, members of the International Set, or retired beer barons—would one look for the "Pilgrims, Wayfarerers, and Travelers" (all professionals, that is) of No. LXXXVII? We recognize the existence, of course, of the scummy creatures talked about in No. LXXXIX, "Maldicenti, Detrattori, e Murmuratori," and we might even admit that some of them work pretty hard at their activities, but we hardly think of them as members of a profession.

Of *bona fide* professions, existent and vanished, the list is long enough to cover just about everything to which the human hand or brain can be turned. And about all of them Garzoni has at least a superficial knowledge which enables him to talk of their first beginnings, of the various branches into which they can be divided, of the tools of the trade, and of other relevant matters. Some of his information, within the range of his limited and sheltered professional experience, comes from his own quick observation; but most of it, there can be little doubt, was gleaned from his reading. It is a little difficult, and perhaps not too charitable, to believe, for instance, that he writes from a firsthand knowledge (if that is the right terminology) on No. LXXIV, "Delle Meretrici, et de' loro seguaci in parte." But with the living examples of Venice, Rome, and Naples before him, it is a little disconcerting to find Garzoni drawing his information and illustrations about the oldest profession from classical writers and their commentators. In the brief "Annotationi" that follow the discourse he cites in this case only three sources, but three of his most-used ones: Celio Rhodigino, Pietro Crinito, and Pietro Vittorio.

Speaking of sources, the "Tavola de gli auttori citati nella presente opera"[20] enumerates 1332 separate authorities. I cannot vouch that Garzoni cites them all in the *Piazza,* but my impression is that he cannot have missed many of them; and he cites some whose names do not appear in the list. Chief among the Italian poets alluded to and quoted are Angelo Poliziano, Andrea Anguillara, Bernardo Tasso, Matteo Boiardo, Cino da Pistoia, Giovanni della Casa, Cecco d'Ascoli, Dante Alighieri, Francesco Petrarca, Giacopo Sannazaro, G.-B. della Porta, "il Giraldi moderno" (= Giraldi Cinthio), G.-B. Pigna, Giovanni Guidiccioni, Marco Girolamo Vida, Lodovico Ariosto, Lodovico Martelli, Giovanni Pontano, Pietro Bembo, Luigi Pulci, Giangiorgio Trissino, Torquato Tasso, Benedetto Varchi, Vittoria Colonna—a sufficiently distinguished roster of names, as we have seen, not unfamiliar to bookish Englishmen of the sixteenth and seventeenth centuries. Omitted from his "Tavola," however, though copiously cited in his other works, is Boccaccio; and Montaigne, with Florio-like inattention to the niceties of identification, is always referred to as "giovan. di Montaigne."

Notwithstanding this impressive array of authorities, and without wishing to minimize Garzoni's real erudition, one suspects that the display is in some sense akin to that factitious one which Cervantes feigns to have been suggested to him for ushering *Don Quijote* "authoritatively" into the world. Garzoni's really effective sources are to be seen in the titles of encyclopedic works repeatedly mentioned in the Annotations. These include, among others, Alessandro d'Alessandro's *Giorni geniali,* Celio Calcagnini's *Tractatus de verborum & rerum,* Celio Rhodigino's *Antiche lettioni,* Pietro Crinito's *De honesta disciplina,* Girolamo Cardano's *De rerum varietate,* Johan Jacob Wecker's *De secretis,* and

---

[20]*Ibid.*, sigs. b2-b3 verso.

Pietro Vittorio's *Varie lettioni.* Such books, along with the *Examen de ingenios* of Juan Huarte, Polydore Vergil's *Degli inventori delle cose* (*De rerum inventoribus*), Pedro Mexia's *Silva de varia lección,* and our own Robert Burton's *Anatomy of Melancholy* give a fairly adequate notion of the genre to which Garzoni's encyclopedic surveys—the *Piazza* preeminently—belong.

Why the kaleidoscopic *Piazza* failed to achieve an English translation remains something of a mystery. That it *was* read and prized in England our cursory examination of Tudor-Stuart libraries has made clear.[21] Florio specifically mentions it in the dedication[22] of his *Worlde of Wordes* as one of several works suggesting that title to him; and Torriano, giving the very title itself, *Piazza universale,* to his collection of Italian proverbs, even more significantly adapts its survey of professions to the pattern of his dialogues forming the supplement to the proverbs. These are, admittedly, small traces to have been left behind by so fascinating and important a book as the *Piazza.* That there are more of them, lurking in obscure or even obvious places, I am reasonably sure. But I must leave their discovery to other searchers.

iii

Garzoni's third major work, *L'Hospidale de' pazzi incurabili,* appeared in 1586.[23] It is a briefer book than the *Theatro*

[21]See above, pp. 36, 44, 47, 57, 58. Copies are also recorded in the libraries represented by Wing *STC* A3166 (in Latin and Italian versions), B1992 (in Latin), B5726 (Burghley's library; in Italian), S2080.

[22]*Worlde of Wordes,* sig. a5: "And as *Tiposcosmia* imaged by *Allessandro Citolini,* and *Fabrica del mondo,* framed by *Francesco Alunno,* and *Piazza universale* set out by *Thomaso Garzoni* tooke their names of the universall worlde, in words to represent things of the world . . . so thought [Florio's Muse] . . ."

[23]*L'Hospidale de' pazzi incurabili nuovamente formato, & posto in luce da Thomaso Garzoni da Bagnacavallo. Con tre Capitoli in Fine Sopra la Pazzia* . . . (Venetia, Gio, Battista Somascho, 1586). Only the third of the *capitoli* is by Garzoni; the first, "à Thomaso Garzoni sopra la Pazzia," is by Theodoro Angelucci, and the second, "In Lode

or the *Piazza* and it quotes fewer poems in its thirty *Discorsi.* Like its predecessors, however, it is heavily charged with learned lore. The wonder is that in a world so full of incurable folly the author feels able to pack all his fools into such narrow quarters. This he is able to accomplish only by crowding a whole company of related fools into each of the wards and by arranging separate quarters for the women. An appended thirty-first discourse, or "Ragionamento," indicates that Eve is no less subject to madness than is Adam. The "Ragionamento" forms, as it were, the obverse of the medal awarded womankind in the *Discorso della nobiltà delle donne.* As the only one of Garzoni's works to be translated into English, and as the only one to receive the distinction of an edition in this century,[24] *L'Hospidale* obviously requires our special attention.

The dedication of *L'Hospidale* is directed, appropriately, to a physician, Bernardino Paterno, whom Garzoni styles "Filosofo clarissimo et Medico eccellentissimo." This is followed by two sonnets of "il Policreti," one in praise of the author and the other on the world's madness. These, in turn, are followed by a "Prologo dell'Auttore a' Spettatori," which terminates the prefatory machinery. Then follow the *Discorsi,* to each of which (except the first and the last) there is by way of novelty annexed a prayer to the tutelary god or goddess of each type of fool. Inasmuch as these are

---

della pazzia," is by the Venetian poet and academician, Guido Casoni. Other editions in Italian: Piacenza, 1586 (G. Bazachi); Ferrara, 1586 (Giulio Cesare Cagnacini & fratelli); Venetia, 1589 (Somascho, in octavo and in quarto), 1594 (Giacomo Antonio Somascho), 1601 (Roberto Meietti); Serravalle di Venetia, 1615 (R. Meglietti); Venetia, 1617, 1652 (T. Baglioni); Lanciano, 1915. An English translation, *The Hospitall of Incurable Fooles* . . . (London, Edm. Bollifant for Edward Blount, 1600), is discussed in the text. French translation: *L'hospital des fols incurables . . . Tiree de l'Italien de Thomas Garzoni, & mise en nostre langue par François de Clarier, sieur de Langval* . . . (Paris, François Iulliot, 1620). In German: *Spital unheylsamer Narren uund Närrinnen, Herrn T.G. Auss der Italiänischen Sprach Teutsch gemacht durch G. F. Messerschmid* (Strassburg, Johann Carolo, 1618).

[24]*L'Hospidale de' pazzi incurabili, a cura di F. Marchionni* (Lanciano, Carabba, 1915).

pagan deities, the treatment is often jocose and the selection of the "patrons" is humorously fitting: Minerva, goddess of wisdom for the raving maniacs; the god Abstemius for drunken fools; Mercury, the fickle, for pretended mad-folk; Hecate for moon-struck wits; Cupid for the love-mad, and so forth. The language is high-flown and exaggerated, the temper halfway between ridicule and pity. Almost always the particular "disease" is illustrated by anecdotal case histories, ancient and modern. Many of these are repeated, with little alteration, from the more extravagant groupings of *cervelli* discussed in the *Theatro*—as are also certain broader themes: melancholia, forgetfulness, malicious vice. The opening Discourse, "Of Madness in General," sets the theme by repeating from Ecclesiastes the motif which marches through most of Garzoni's writing: *Stultorum infinitus est numerus*. At the end of the discourses are three *capitoli* on madness.

The English translator, whoever he was,[25] produced a version which is reasonably close to the original, both in letter and in spirit. His title page, needlessly apologetic and at once perceptive of Garzoni's underlying structural metaphor, reads thus: *The Hospitall of Incurable Fooles: Erected in English, as neer the first Italian modell and platforme, as the unskilful hand of an ignorant Architect could devise . . . Printed by Edm. Bollifant for Edward Blount*. 1600. He has added, as title-page motto, "I pazzi, é li prudenti, fanno giustissima bilancia"—"Fools and wise men balance out," a more generous attitude than that of Garzoni, for whom the wise are always outweighed; and he has had the wit to sign himself, at the end of an added prefatory epistle, "Il pazzissimo," "the maddest wit of all." Of the preliminary materials in the original

---

[25]The translation has been attributed both to Edward Blount, whose name appears on the title page as publisher, and to Thomas Nashe. I have been able to trace but a single copy of this translation in English Libraries of our period: in the auction catalogue of Francis Bernard's (1627-1698) library (= Wing B1992), casually tucked away in the Appendix, Bundle XVII, is, among others, No. 27. *Hospital of Incurable Fools.*

he preserves only the "Prologue of the Author to the behold-ers,"[26] and he does not translate the terminal *capitoli*. Remem-bering that Fortune favors fools, he substitutes for Garzoni's dedication one directed "To the good old Gentlewoman, and her special Benefactresse, Madam Fortune! [to whom] Dame Folly (Matron of the Hospitall) makes curte-sie, and speakes as followeth." The publisher, if he is not also the translator, adds another of similarly facetious tenor, "To my most neere and Capriccious Neighbor, ycleped *John Hodgson,* alias *John Hatter,* or (as some will) John of Paules Churchyard, (*Cum multis aliis, quaenunc imprimere longum est:*) Edward Blount, *wisheth prosperous successe in his Monomachie, with the French and Spaniard.*" In this, with good-humored persiflage, he appoints Hodgson, "John of all Johns," to act as "Patron or Treasurer" of this "guest-house," requiring him to "sweare to the uttermost of your en-devours, without fraude or imposture to releeve and cherish all such creatures as are by the hand of Fortune committed to your custodie. . . So helpe you a fat Capon and the Contents of this Booke."[27]

Something of the translator's modesty and wit may appear in the following excerpt from his address entitled "Not to the wise Reader":

> Well, having in this Hospitall received so good com-fort, and succour my selfe; in religious charitie I could not but make knowne unto you this worthie Italian worke, framed peradventure upon their yeere of Jubilee, or grace, and therefore propounded in generall to all men, for reliefe and cure of their giddie maladies. I crave no pardon of my errors or faults (yet are they many, and onely mine owne) beeing but a Foole, in reporting to Fooles what an other hath censured of humaine folly: . . . this I did carelessly, accept you of it as lightly. Yet consider what patience you have with the wine you drink in Tavernes, and beleeve me (as a poore Traveller) it is all exceedingly bastardiz'd from his originall purity: and even your Phisicall drams, that

---

[26]*Hospitall,* sigs. A3-A4 verso.
[27]*Ibid.,* "The Epistle Dedicatorie."

are so greedily sought after, suffer a little sophistication by the hands of the Apothecarie. Thinke not much therefore, if so tickle and foolish a commoditie as this is, be somewhat endamaged by the transportation of it out of Italy, but making some pleasant and profitable collection out of the same, let us leave all preeminence of folly to themselves, as I ascribe all due reward and demerite to my originall Author.[28]

How little the commodity was "endamaged by the transportation of it out of Italy" a few further observations may help to make clear. Except for the omission of the verses and the free rehandling of prefatory material, the substance and order of Garzoni's *Hospidale* are duly followed. Unlike Figueroa's Spanish adaptation of the *Piazza,* which omits nearly a third of the discourses and Hispanizes freely, even to the extent of substituting Spanish poets for those cited by Garzoni, this is a genuine translation. Here and there, it is true, the Englishman will miss the meaning or fumble an allusion, as when he mistakes the Italian "l'essempio di quel Monferrino"[29] for a reference to a specific person named Monferrino; or when, in Discourse IV, he turns Garzoni's "Messer Dante" into *John Dante.*[30] Such gratuitous mistakes are few. But it is true, also, that he occasionally attempts to give Garzoni's illustrations an English name and local habitation, as may be seen in his rendering of the following brief passage describing an encounter between a discreet Venetian senator and a loud-mouthed know-it-all ninny-hammer:

. . . e addimandato da che luogo fosse, et intendendo [il Senatore] ch'era da Portia, & del suo nome, intendendo c'haveva nome il Cavezza, prendendolo destramente per il cavezzo, disse queste parole: Sier grugno di Portia quanto vi staria bene una cavezza, tornate di gratia a Portia se non volete devenire una brasuola, per le quali parole, scottato, & camuffo tornò al compagno, & disse, andiamo di gratia via, che quel gentil'

---

[28]*Ibid.*, sig. a2 recto-verso.
[29]*Hospidale,* "Discorso VII," p. 20b.
[30]*Hospitall,* p. 23.

huomo c'havete visto, m'ha detto nell'orecchia che c'è pena di tre tratti di corda a chi sta sù questa porta.[31]

The untranslatable punning and wordplay of this delightful spoofery is thus conveyed in the English:

> . . . being by the Senatour demaunded, of whence he was, being given to understand that he was of Portia, as also knowing that his surname was *Cavezza* (or Horse-collar) taking him quickly by the collar, hee used these wordes: Master Grunt of Hoggenorton, although an halter woulde well become you, yet I praie you returne againe to your towne of Porkington, except you means to become a collop of bacon: through which wordes, bedawed and gulled as he was, he returned to his companion, and saide, come for gods sake let us be gone, for the gentleman you saw told me in my eare, that there is a penaltie set downe, of three twitches with a cord, for any that shall stand gaping at this gate.[32]

That the translator was reasonably conversant with the Italian tongue will be quickly apparent to anyone who takes the pain to compare the English and original texts. But it will also appear from such a comparison—as, in part, it does from this present passage—that the translator, like Ben Jonson,[33] relied on Florio's *Worlde of Wordes* to get him through the rougher places. Florio defines *Cavezza* as both "halter" and "horse collar"; *Grugnare* as "to grunt as a hog," and *Grugno di porco* (Garzoni's "Sier Grugno di Portia") as "a hogs snout"; *Brasuole* as "steakes, *collops,* rashers, or carbonados"; *Camuffo* as "a man . . . made a foole or a *gull*"; *Scottare* as "to scalde, to burne, to parch, to sing[e]"—but, just above that applicable definition, *Scótta,* "a chough or a dawe," which was what caught the translator's eye; and *Tratti di córda*—the whole phrase entered—as "strappadoes given with a corde."

---

[31]*Hospidale,* "Discorso XXVIII," p. 64a.
[32]*Hospitall,* p. 127.
[33]See Mario Praz, *Machiavelli in Inghilterra ed altri saggi* (Roma, 1943), 2nd ed., pp. 173-192.

In neither the translation nor the original is there any pronounced attitude of sympathy for the victims of mental imbalance or emotional disturbances, though an occasional word of commiseration may slip almost unheeded from the pen: "grievous malady," "these poore bransickes, and witlesse men," "weakelings, deprived of all helpe and advise," "the poore stupide, & Forlorne Fooles,"[34] and so on. More commonly the epithets and other descriptive labels suggest ridicule or aversion: the inmates of the Hospital are cockscombs, dolts, "giddie-headed Pyes," "harebrained and forgetfull Fooles," "Oxe-heads," "ninnies,"[35] "dull-pated-Calfes," "dottrells and shallow-pated Fooles," "dizzards," "buzzards," "Bergamascan blockheads," "nyddicockes," "buffles," "lob-lollies," "fantasticks," "peevish Pouljob-hams," "doddipoules," "lunatickes," "carpet fools," "heteroclite, reverse, thwart, and headstrong Fooles," "gog-furies," "scoffing and jesting fools" (otherwise known as "frivolous chatterers" or "Fabulanians"), "buffones," "testie & fustian Fooles," "outragious, fel, and Bedlam Fooles," "grosse and three elbowed Fooles," "unbridled fools" (these include Aretino, Franco, Burchiello, and Berni),[36] and *Matti Torlurú* (Discorso X), whom the translator calls "senselesse and giddie-headed Fooles" and Florio defines as "a fool, a ninnie, a giddie-headed gull." As we survey this motley crew and watch their mad antics, so like some of our own and those of our college students nowadays, we seem to hear, beneath the ruckus, the mocking music of one of Shakespeare's wiser fools:

Lord, what mortals these fools be!

The spectacle of madness was for our ancestors something of a penny peep show, and Bedlam and other madhouses were visited for diversion. This is the prevailing temper of

---

[34] *Hospitall*, pp. 9, 13, 20, 36, respectively.
[35] Celebrated, a few years later, in Robert Armin's *A Nest of Ninnies* (London, 1608).
[36] *Hospitall*, p. 127.

the madhouse scenes in certain of our early dramas: in the festivous baiting of Malvolio in Shakespeare's *Twelfth Night,* in the macabre Websterian *Duchess of Malfi,* and, above all, in the prison tour of Middleton's *The Changeling.* It is precisely this note which is struck at the end of Garzoni's *Prologo dell'Auttore a' Spettatori* and faithfully rendered in the English translation:

> Whosoever therefore wil go into these pastimes, he shal pay at least a peece of twenty for his part, for this is no two-penie matter. . . . The first thing shewed, shall be a monster with many heads [i.e., "Of Follie in generall: the first discourse"], who with his deformity shall make everie one amased, neither were *Hydra, Medusa, or Python* so dreadfull and horrible as he will be: And then one after another you shall see the palace of the Witch *Alcina,* chamber by chamber, full of people enchanted in braine, and transformed with brutish Metamorphoses into unreasonable and sottish folke, where betweene laughter & admiration, everie one shal thinke his nine-pence well spent, departing well satisfied with the Author, who with new Magicke will hereafter represent unto you the castle of *Atlas* full of Dawcocks, and he will labour to conduct you thither in safety by *Logistilla,* giving you *Angelicaes* ring in your hand, by meane whereof, discovering other mens follies, you may shew your selves the wiser. But now retire a little while the monster is loosed, & fixe your eies steedfastly upon him, if you will woonder at the first sight.[37]

The varied manifestations of madness treated by Garzoni, and especially that depressive melancholia to which he repeatedly gives attention[38] should make his works, one would think, an obvious hunting ground for those who seriously discuss the mad folk of Elizabethan drama and the eccentrics anatomized by Timothy Bright and Robert Burton. Yet, as

---

[37]*Ibid.,* sig. A4 verso.
[38]*Hospidale,* Discorso III; *Theatro,* Discorso XLVII; *Sinagoga,* Discorso XI; *Serraglio,* Appartamento de' Sogni, Stanza Quinta, pp. 392-395.

far as I can find, only one scholar, Professor Lawrence Babb, has even so much as suggested that Garzoni's *Hospidale,* not to mention his other writings, may lurk in the background of such notable English productions as *The Anatomy of Melancholy* and "Il Penseroso."[39] And no one, again so far as I am aware, has aligned with its obvious inspiration that tongue-in-cheek later proposal of the sanest madman of them all, the *Serious and Useful Scheme to make an Hospital for Incurables* of Jonathan Swift.[40]

You will look in vain for any mention of Garzoni in the standard histories of medicine or science, but this application of the silent treatment does not mean that he does not belong there. His preoccupation with magic, wonders, and pseudo-science in general in his *Theatro, Piazza,* and *Serraglio,* as well as his clear-cut venturings into an incipient psychiatry in this *Hospitall of Incurable Fools* entitle him to such a place. In view of this past neglect it is surprising but not without significance, I think, that the National Library of Medicine in Bethesda should possess four editions of the *Hospidale* (including the English translation) and two of the *Theatro de' vari, e diversi cervelli.* If we live long enough and make a proper use of our own unaddled *cervelli,* we may yet catch up with the past.

---

[39]See Lawrence Babb, *The Elizabethan Malady* (East Lansing, 1951), pp. 36*n,* 40*n,* 44; and his article, "The Background of 'Il Penseroso,'" *Studies in Philology,* XXXVII (1940), 257 ff.

[40]See *The Works of Jonathan Swift,* ed. Sir Walter Scott, 19 vols. (London, 1883), IX, 314-337.

Swift's library contained relatively few Italian books. Relying on the evidence in the essay and the reprint of the sale catalogue provided by Harold Williams, *Dean Swift's Library* (Cambridge [Eng.], 1932), it would not appear that he owned any of Garzoni's works. His Machiavelli, Tasso, and Davila (*Cat.,* Nos. 374, 449, 594) are in English; he has Sarpi's *Concilio Tridentino* in Italian and in French (*Cat.,* Nos. 252, 232), a Florio Dictionary (*Cat.* 205), four Italian MSS. (*Cat.* 545-548), and a pre-Diodati Italian Bible (*Cat.* 357). At one time he had a Diodati Bible (*Essay,* p. 40) and a collection of Bentivoglio's *Lettere* (Essay, p. 69 *n*).

iv

The *Sinagoga de gl'Ignoranti* was the last of Garzoni's secular works to be published during his lifetime, and the one that made the least impression upon his contemporaries.[41] Like its predecessors, it makes a conspicuous display of learning, mostly classical, for there is but little citing of modern writers. A preliminary *Tavola* lists the names of only 140 "auttori, i cui nomi sono citati." The *Sinagoga* proceeds by the usual method of definition, division, and illustration through its sixteen discourses and reaches the not wholly unexpected conclusion that learning is more virtuous than ignorance. Its overwhelming vapidity and lack of inspiration is partially reflected in the opening remarks of the final *Discorso:*

> Having in the preceding Discourses depicted the qualities, manners, and peculiarities of the ignorant, with all their conduct and demeanor, there can be no doubt that the curious reader should desire in the end to hear about the triumphs and glories of this sapless and witless mother of all the vices and shortcomings of the world; of whom, for all those showy capers, can only be recorded a most solemn pomp of infamy, so that she may be rewarded in that fashion which appears to be appropriate to her special merits.

Possibly the most interesting feature of the *Sinagoga* is reserved for the final three pages, which are devoted entirely to a deliberate "puff" for one of Garzoni's "forthcoming" books —it has been forthcoming since the days of the *Piazza*[42]— his *Palazzo de gl'Incanti*. This work did not appear in his

---

[41]*La Sinagoga de gl'ignoranti nuovamente formata, & posta in luce* (Venetia, Gio. Battista Somasco, 1589). Other editions in Italian: Pavia, 1589 (Andrea Viani); Venetia, 1594 (Giacomo Antonio Somasco), 1601 (Roberto Meietti), 1604 (Giacomo Ant. Somasco); Serravalle di Venetia, 1605 (Roberto Meglietti), 1617. In Spanish: *El theatro de ingenios y Sinagoga de ignorantes, de Thomas Garçon . . . Puesto en español por Iayme Rebullosa . . .* (Barcelona, Iayme Cendrat, 1600).

[42]See *Piazza universale,* Discorso 3 (Annotationi), 39, 41.

lifetime, or under this title, but was published much later by his brother Bartolomeo. In the interval there also appeared posthumously another work of a very curious sort, the *Mirabile cornucopia consolatorio,* which we must bypass for the moment in order to visit Garzoni's *Palace of Enchantments.* Magicians stronger than those that bedeviled Don Quijote have been at work upon it, for before we reach the entrance they have already changed it from a palace to a *Serraglio,*[43] or enclosed garden. Under its disguise it appears as *Il Serraglio de gli stupori del mondo,* and the reason for the transmogrification is explained by both the editor and the publisher of the new volume. After listing his departed brother's publications, Bartolomeo adds: "He busied himself beyond these in composing other works, but chiefly the present one promised by him under the name of *Palace.* But, this title having been used by another with little happy result, it has seemed best to me, considering the principal matters treated in it, to re-style it *The Enclosure of the Amazements of the World.*"[44] So far the Very Reverend Father Don Bartolomeo. Now hear the industrious and money-minded publisher:

---

[43]*Il Serraglio de gli Stupori del Mondo, di Tomaso Garzoni da Bagnacavallo. Diviso in Diece Appartamenti, secondo gli vari, & ammirabili oggetti.*

Cioé di	*Mostri,*	*Sibille,*
	Prodigii,	*Sogni,*
	Prestigii,	*Curiosità Astrologica,*
	Sorti,	*Miracoli in Genere, e*
	Oracoli,	*Maraviglie in Spetie,*

Narrate da' più celebri Scrittori, e descritte da' più famosi Historici, e Poeti, le quali talhora occorrono, considerandosi la loro probabilità, overo improbabilità secondo la natura. Opera non meno dotta, che curiosa, cosi per Theologi, Predicatori, Scritturisti, e Legistici: come per Filosofi, Academici, Astrologi, Historici, Poeti, & altri. Arricchita di varie Annotationi dal M.R.P.D. Bartolomeo Garzoni suo Fratello, Prelato di Santo Ubaldo d'Ugubbio, e Teologo Privilegiato della Congregatione Lateranense. Con tre copiosissime tavole. Et Licenza de' Superiori, e Privilegi (Venetia, Ambrosio, et Bartolomeo Dei, 1613).

[44]*Serraglio,* sig. bl.

Garzoni, a Wit so rare and so distinguished that his fame will pass down to all posterity illustrious and shining, left behind at his decease various and diverse works no less exalted than curious in nature, so that by all the informed they have been most highly desired. Nor is there anyone who will greatly marvel that in so many years after his death they have not yet seen the light, for such are the stumbling-blocks of the world that sometimes it is requisite to hold back that most spurred on by a heated desire. Nor is that reason inconsiderable that it behooves us to accommodate ourselves to the times and not to depart from the prescriptions of the Superiors. Whence, as for that great Palace—promised and re-promised—what could be done about it if so much of the matter therein tossed about was displeasing to the Superiors when laid bare in the common speech?

The reader is not to despair, however. The public-spirited publisher has stirred his stumps and Don Bartolomeo has stirred *his,* and all has finally been adjusted to the satisfaction of those blessed Superiors, so that now the patient and long-expectant reader may feast on the ambrosia of an even daintier banquet than that supplied in the same author's *Piazza universale.* As for the title under which he has been all this while expecting it, the new title of the book is distinctly superior,

> and the more so in that, having seen the unhappy success of a Book printed under the title of *Palace of Enchantments,* at my insistence the *Palace* of Garzoni has been changed to this *Enclosure of Amazements,* and that after duly considering both the failure of that other book and the important, unusual, and most useful matters which are treated of in this one. So behold here satisfied your every desire; flourish, gentlemen; and I shall visit you again shortly with other books greatly to your content and consolation.[45]

The "unfortunate" book mentioned by both the editor and

---

[45]*Ibid.,* sig. b2 recto-verso.

the publisher was Strozzi Cigogna's *Palagio de gl'Incanti,*[46] a fat quarto which contained only four of a proposed forty-five books. The matters treated in it were indeed similar to those in Garzoni's book; but Cigogna seems to have taken from Garzoni only the catchy title—perhaps at the instigation of *his* publisher, Roberto Meietti, who in the same year, 1605, issued the *Sinagoga* in a collective edition of Garzoni's works. The presence of at least one copy of the *Palagio* in England[47] is possibly the result of the advance publicity in the *Sinagoga* or the *Piazza universale.*

Garzoni's *Serraglio,* over which we must not linger, is a big book, on the order of his earlier *Piazza.* It houses the ten topics of its discussion—monsters, prodigies, illusions, fortunes, oracles, sybils, dreams, astrological secrets, miracles, marvelous happenings—in forty-two *stanze,* or chambers, and supports the agglomerative mass of credulity and misinformation by the citation of no fewer than 642 "authorities." It is hardly possible to disengage Garzoni's learning (and folly) from those of the intermeddling brother, whose initials in the margin are supposed to indicate *his* contribution; but of none of his books is it truer that, as one critic says of the *Piazza,*[48] Garzoni's is an "ingegno bizzarro e poco costruttivo."

We come, finally, to that other posthumously published work, the *Mirabile cornucopia,*[49] mentioned earlier. This is the briefest and, even when we have begun to expect oddities from him, the most surprising performance of our Canon

---

[46]Strozzi Cigogna (or Cicogna), *Del palagio de gl'incanti & delle gran meraviglie de gli spiriti, & di tutta la natura loro* . . . (Vicenza, ad istanza di Roberto Meglietti, 1605).

[47]See above, p. 38. There was also a Latin version, copies of which have been traced to the libraries of Richard Smith, Wing STC S4151 (1682); Dr. Thomas Jacomb, Wing J113 (1687); and the bookseller, Robert Scott, Wing S2080 (1687/8).

[48]Carlo Cordié, in *Dizionario letterario Bompiani delle opere e dei personaggi di tutti i tempi e di tutte le letterature* (Milano, 1957), vol. V, s.v. "Piazza universale."

[49]*Il Mirabile cornucopia consolatorio di Thomaso Garzoni da Bagnacavallo. Discorso nuovo, vago, e dotto, ne più dato in luce* (Bologna, Heredi di Giovanni Rossi, 1601).

Regular. It is cast in the form of a consolatory epistle and is in substance a mock encomium of cuckoldry. Does his Bolognese friend lament the unfaithfulness of his wife and pity himself for having to wear horns and suffer the name of cuckold? Let him change his way of thinking, then, for he ought

> rather to take comfort with himself, or better, to consider himself most honored, being thus classed as "horned," this designation being (as he will see, reading this discourse of mine) a name the most celebrated and famous that one could possibly say. . . .[50]

And so he runs through a series of ridiculous arguments and illustrations to show the antiquity, ubiquity, and dignity of horns. Nature, he says, creating animals of singular distinction, has made them horned—witness the unicorn. Names, he says, are rendered famous by the men who bear them; the *cornuti* can look to such names as Cornazzano, Ascanio della Corna, and the Bolognese Ascanio dal Cornetto. Many ancient families, Roman and Italian, have names that memorialize some form of "the horn."[51] Geography, seafaring, hunting, war, religion, every aspect of man's life, are called upon to show the dignity of the horn.[52] The very curls anciently worn, and even now worn by Venetian ladies, to decorate their lovely brows are called "horns."[53] The heavens themselves bear horned signs: the Ram, Capricorn, Taurus. Even the Moon, in certain phases, is described as "horned." Moreover, the Ancients had certain horned gods, etc., etc.[54] It is all very corny; and if we had not already, with Sir Philip Sidney, been "a peece of a *logician* before [we] came to him," he might almost have persuaded us to wish ourselves the head and horns of Actaeon.

In Garzoni's house it never rains but it pours. Hear how he

---

[50]*Cornucopia*, p. 7.
[51]*Ibid.*, pp. 8-14.
[52]*Ibid.*, pp. 14-28.
[53]*Ibid.*, p. 18.
[54]*Ibid.*, pp. 30-33.

puts the final polish to the horns that have sprouted on his friend's forehead:

> Finally, your Most Magnificient Lordship (or Horn-ship) should note, to give good measure to the praises of horns, that among the Egyptian and Hebrew caba-lists they were never other than the symbol of great and worthy things, of grace, of pleasantness, of mercy, of magnificence, of happiness, of concord, of gaiety, of power, of wealth, and of righteous sternness. Hence, he who has bestowed upon your Most Exalted Lord-ship the title of *Cornuto* wished to imply nothing other than that you are pleasant, merciful, strong, righteous, splendid, happy, peace-loving, merry, and prepared to bare your teeth against him if he had injured you by any other name.[55]

With the amorous adventures of Pepys in real life and with the Restoration stage renderings of the Art and Craft of Cuckoldry in the background—Wycherley's Horner may stand as enigmatic emblem of an entire social milieu—it would be a worse than Garzonian madness to think seriously that the English had anything to learn from the Italians about horns. Nevertheless, there was published in 1661 a little English *jeu d'esprit* which seems to indicate as much. I refer to George Rogers' *The Horn Exalted, or, Room for Cuckolds*.[56] This is conducted quite in the spirit[57] of Garzoni's mock eulogy, uses the word *cornucopia* for "cuckold's house," uses

---

[55]*Ibid.*, p. 35.

[56]I cite the second edition, *The Horn Exalted. Or, Room for Cuck-olds. Being a Treatise concerning the Reason and Original of the Word Cuckold, and why such are said to wear Horns. . . . Also an Appendix Concerning Women and Jealousy . . .* (London, 1721). This edition carries an engraved frontispiece showing in the fore-ground a well-antlered man surrounded by a unicorn, a stag, an ele-phant, a horned owl, and other horned animals, while a horned moon rides in the heavens. I trace one copy of this work: [Richard Smith,] *Bibliotheca Smithiana: sive Catalogus Librorum* . . . [London,] 1682; p. 203, No. 442. (Wing *STC*, S4151).

[57]*E.g., The Horn Exalted,* p. 15: "Horns ought not to be so vilified, since of old they were in Honour, and some think the Beginning of Horns came from the *Indians,* whom *Homer* and others esteemed as Friends of the Gods."

many of the Italian's illustrations, including the unicorn, the elephant, the horned altars of the ancients, the "horns" or curls worn in women's headdresses, the horned moon, the horned signs of the Zodiac, and so on.[58] It even cites copiously from an alleged Italian work on the subject, called (not very credibly) *L. Cornuito del modio*,[59] which, if it exists, I have been unable to identify. My guess is that it is either a pure fabrication, or else derived from Garzoni. It is most unlikely that so many correspondences of illustration and spirit should exist between the two works if there were not some thread of connection.[60]

Facete, bizarre, mildly pessimistic, endlessly inquisitive, omniumgatherumnic, enormously learned, seasoned with ancient saws and apt quotations, given to Rabelaisian conceits and splurges of language, the works of Tomaso Garzoni of Bagnacavallo must have been to English palates quite as toothsome a dainty as they were to an Italian bracing himself for the plunge into a full-blown *secentesimo*. I refuse to believe that he entirely deserves the almost complete oblivion from which I have tried momentarily to lift him. We English-speaking people owe to Bagnacavallo something more than a footnote reminding us that Byron's Allegra is buried there.

---

[58]*Ibid.*, pp. 12, 20; 19; 16, 19; 14, 20; 39; 14, 23; 22-23.

[59]*Ibid.*, pp. 11-19.

[60]*The Horn Exalted* has the distinction, not too common at the time, of containing frequent allusions to and quotations from both Chaucer and Spenser.

INDEX

Abbott, George, Archbishop of Canterbury, 27, 29

Acontius, Jacobus. *See* Aconzio, Giacopo

Aconzio, Giacopo, 5*n*, 15

Adair, E. R., 6*n*

Adriano, Alfonso, 53

Aglionby, William, translator, 21

Agnello, G. B., 5*n*

Agrippa, Camillo, 37

Alamanni, Luigi, 50

Alberti, Leone Battista, 50, 55

Alberti, Oliviero, printer, 73*n*

Alciato, Andrea, 70

Aldi, Italian printers, 3

d'Alessandro, Alessandro, 77

Alexis of Piedmont. *See* Ruscelli Girolamo

Alunno, Francesco, 49, 50, 54, 57, 78*n*

Amadis de Gaula, 55

Ammirato, Scipione, 57

Andreini, Isabella, 38, 75

Anatomy of Melancholy (Burton), 86

Angelucci, Teodoro, 78*n*

Anguillara, Giovanni Andrea dell', 50, 70, 71*n*, 77

Annesley, Arthur, Earl of Anglesey, 57

Annibale tragicomedia, 60

Antonielli, Antoniello degli (pseudonym of John Wolfe), 21

Arber, Edward, 14*n*, 30*n*

Architecture, 50, 51

Aretino, Pietro, 17-20, 30, 34, 35, 38, 41, 50, 52, 55, 58, 59, 61, 63, 70

Ariosto, Lodovico, 30, 35, 36, 38, 41, 45, 50, 57, 58, 59, 62, 70, 71*n*, 75, 77

Armin, Robert, 84*n*

Arundel, Earl of. *See* Fitzalan, Henry

Astolfi, Giovanni, 38

Atterbury, Lewis, 29*n*

Aurellio, Giovanni Battista, 16*n*

Babb, Lawrence, 86, 86*n*

Bacon, Sir Francis, 27-28, 38*n*, 48, 58

Baglioni, Tomaso, printer, 79*n*

Bald, R. C., 27*n*

Bandello, Matteo, 53, 59

Barbagrigia. *See* Blado, Antonio

Barezzi, Barezzo ("il Barezzo"), printer, 73*n*

Bargagli, Scipione, 50

Barlement, Noel, 8

Barnes, Joseph, Oxford printer, 5, 7, 24, 35

Baronio, Cesare, 59

Barozzi da Vignola, Giacomo, 51*n*

Bartley, Elizabeth, 34*n*

Bartoli, Daniello, 58

Basse, William, 38*n*

Bazachi, G., printer, 79*n*

Beaumont, Francis, 40

Bedell, William, 29

Bello, N. *See* Lundorp, M. C.

Bembo, Pietro, 35, 38, 41, 50, 57, 62, 70, 71*n*, 77

Bengodi, fictitious place of publication, 19, 55*n*

Bentivoglio, Ercole, 46, 75

95